Connecting with Socially Isolated Seniors

Connecting with Socially Isolated Seniors

A Service Provider's Guide

Patricia Osage

with Mary McCall

Foreword by Harry R. Moody

HPP
Health Professions Press

Baltimore • Sydney • London

Health Professions Press

Health Professions Press, Inc.
Post Office Box 10624
Baltimore, Maryland 21285-0624

www.healthpropress.com

Interior and cover designs by Mindy Dunn.
Typeset by Mindy Dunn.
Manufactured in the United States of America by Versa Press, East Peoria,
Illinois.

Photographers: Asha Beene (pp. 19, 43, 66, 73, 68); Katrina Bill (pp. 21, 98);
Dorothy Cervantes (pp. 38, 46, 85, 99); Clare Hannemann (pp. 1, 65, 89, 103);
Troy Herrington (p. 95); Lyrika Ho (p. 75); Kim Khuc (p. 111); Amy Layne (p. 35);
Roy Manzanares (pp. 27, 99); Iris Mazaroff (cover, pp. 3, 57); Anita Missin (p. ii);
Hang Mosier (p. 51); Patricia Osage (pp. 60, 77, 83, 115); Kit Solowy (p. 11).

All photographs feature Satellite Housing residents, staff, and volunteers and
are used with permission.

Library of Congress Cataloging-in-Publication Data

Osage, Patricia.
  Connecting with socially isolated seniors : a service provider's guide / by
Patricia Osage ; with Mary McCall.
     p. ; cm.
  Includes bibliographical references.
  ISBN 978-1-932529-73-9 (pbk.)
  I. McCall, Mary E., 1960– II. Title.
  [DNLM: 1. Mental Health Services. 2. Social Isolation. 3. Aged. 4. Health
Services for the Aged. 5. Housing for the Elderly. 6. Risk Factors. WT 145]

362.198'97–dc23

2012008904

British Library Cataloguing in Publication data are available from the British
Library.

This is dedicated to all service coordinators of affordable senior housing. Few can ever really know the depth of knowledge, the emotional strength, and the compassion it takes to perform this job well every day.

And to Iris Mazaroff, who has spent more than 40 years of her life working to prevent and alleviate social isolation among seniors.

Contents

About Satellite Housing

This book comes out of years of expertise and experience of the staff and residents of Satellite Housing, Inc., which provides affordable, service-enriched housing to the San Francisco East Bay's lowest-income seniors. A nonprofit development agency, Satellite has won awards for its housing design for deaf seniors as well as for its sustainable building practices. Established in 1966, its portfolio consists of more than 1,800 primarily rent-subsidized apartments across 28 affordable housing communities that serve 1,650 people.

Satellite Housing's developments are located in a broad range of communities, serving as anchors in low-income urban neighborhoods and advancing income integration and diversity in affluent suburban areas. Each development is financed through creative public and private partnerships between federal and local government agencies as well as commercial banks and investors.

Each Satellite Housing property is staffed with individuals who are committed to providing the highest quality of services and housing to residents in addition to supporting their physical, spiritual, and emotional health. Satellite's core values include the following beliefs:

- To be healthy and happy, every person needs a home.

- Along with housing, services and support must be provided to best assist residents.

About the Authors

Patricia Osage is the Director of Resident Services at Satellite Housing in Berkeley, California. She has worked for over 22 years in various human services capacities, including 2 years at a primary health care clinic in Yemen. Osage has performed direct case management for a number of different demo-  graphic and special needs groups, and ran the services department at the Tenderloin Housing Clinic in San Francisco before coming to Satellite Housing. She is an expert in the field of supportive services for formerly homeless adults and low-income seniors and frequently provides national and local presentations on topics related to best practices within these service fields.

Osage runs Satellite Housing's large services department, which consists of three major components: wheelchair accessible transit, nonclinical case management, and activities programming. She has developed extensive programs within civic engagement and intergenerationally-based contexts to provide low-income seniors with a wide range of opportunities for involvement in their communities.

With her staff, Osage collaboratively developed a unique model of working with residents that addresses the goals of optimal health, financial stability, and individual well-being and purposeful living. The long-term goals that encompass all three are for seniors to be able to not only *age in place*, but also *thrive in their community*.

Mary McCall, Ph.D., professor of psychology at St. Mary's College of California, is an expert in aging and values-based decision-making on the part of individuals and families regarding issues such as long-term care and the death of an older adult. Professor McCall explores the social policies of housing, health, and  support services for low-income seniors, as well as the role of cultural values in social policies around the world regarding aging.

Acknowledgments

This guidebook would not have been possible without the AmeriCorps VISTA program. The Corporation for National and Community Service brings much-needed attention and resources to the growing issue of seniors in poverty; for that, we are forever grateful. Our first VISTA member was Kaitlin Carmody, who tirelessly pored over books and research and scribbled down hundreds of people's ideas to glean as much as she could about the current beliefs and facts around social isolation. Carmella Fleming, our second-year VISTA member, flew out from Iowa and immediately dove into the project with full enthusiasm. She spent long hours perfecting the original design and format for the book and readying it for distribution by Satellite Housing. The hard work of both of these women will have lasting impacts on many.

A special thank you to the hundreds of Satellite Housing residents who responded to the survey regarding social networks and to the many residents who participated in lengthy roundtable discussions. And thanks to all of the Satellite service coordinators and activities coordinators who opened up to share stories, struggles, and successes. You have been invaluable to the creation of this book. Your head-on commitment to seeking good lives for Satellite's low-income seniors provides me with hope for the world.

And last but not least, thanks to Katrina Bill, Iris Mazaroff, and Asha Beene for bringing to life the stories of Satellite Housing residents who overcame social isolation. Thanks to those residents who so generously allowed us to print your stories. Finally, our immense thanks go to Professor Mary McCall for her eternal belief in the power of research and the power of sharing its findings!

Patricia Osage

Foreword

ISOLATION AND THE GIFTS OF AGE

If we live long enough, we will face the challenge of isolation. I learned this firsthand from Larry Morris, a dear friend of our family who moved in with us at age 90 and died in our midst at the age of 97. By the end, Larry had outlived two wives (he had no children) and countless friends. Yet, by any imaginable standard, his life reached its end, not in loneliness, but in the fullness of time and love. When I think of Larry I'm reminded of how he advised me that the secret to successful aging was to make new friends, especially younger friends.

Financial planners speak of a "longevity risk," namely, the threat of outliving our savings. In terms of our social lives, there is also a longevity risk: outliving those we love. Alas, I recognize this even at the tender age of 67. I have lost dear friends whose lives and memories can never be replaced. Yet tragedy, and even isolation, need not bring the loss of meaning. This is a lesson we must never forget, lest we fall into despair about old age.

Addressing the challenge of isolation in old age must come from two sides: from within ourselves and from those around us. Larry Morris was enriched by the fact that he was able have dinner with us each night, that he could have our small children playing at his feet. Help came from not only those around him, but also from his own sense of purpose in life. Staying connecting socially is also essential.

"Only connect!" wrote E. M. Forster (*Howard's End*), and his advice still stands. Today opportunities to keep people connected, from Skype to Facebook, have never been more abundant. Modern forms of staying connected, however, are no substitute for a deeper investment in the lives of others. Despite our connections, despite conviviality and volunteerism, we live in a world where more of us are at risk of social isolation as more of us reach advanced age and outlive those we love.

The answer to this challenge requires that we "get by with a little help from our friends," including those who work in community-based and residential senior housing. This insightful guidebook, *Connecting with Socially Isolated Seniors,* offers many useful tips for how service providers can explore the needs of seniors who live alone in the community and identify and assist those who are at risk of social isolation. Based on decades of experience working with residents living in senior housing, Patricia Osage outlines several risk factors for social isolation and highlights specific suggestions for how to intervene. Those assisting seniors to thrive in community will find *Connecting with Socially Isolated Seniors* to be an invaluable resource.

But something else is required to address the risks of social isolation, not from outside but from within ourselves as we grow older. It is beautifully conveyed by Florida Scott-Maxwell in *The Measure of My Days,* a journal composed in a nursing home. There she writes: "Age puzzles me. I thought it was a quiet time. My seventies were interesting, and fairly serene, but my eighties are passionate. I grow more intense as I age. To my own surprise I burst out with hot conviction. Only a few years ago I enjoyed my tranquility; now I am so disturbed by the outer world and by human quality in general that I want to put things right, as though I still owed a debt to life." "Owing a debt to life" constitutes our response to the challenge of longevity, to "outliving the self," and so finding purpose and meaning in our lives.

I read those words in the copy of a book owned by Larry Morris, which he left to me, as with so many other gifts. Can we find ways to offer, and to receive, the gifts of age?

Harry R. Moody
Vice President and Director of Academic Affairs, AARP

Preface

Over the years at Satellite Housing, as we rolled out increasingly rich programs and fine-tuned the quality of service delivery, the primary issue that we couldn't quite overcome was engaging the harder-to-reach seniors. Staff members had stories here and there of successful, creative techniques to prevent or reduce social isolation while working with one type of senior, but many staff members would find themselves baffled when they worked with another type of individual. There was, however, no consolidated information about best practices available for people like us concerned with this widespread issue. The need for a book like this one was voiced repeatedly. We all saw (or didn't see but knew about) a significant number of individuals who rarely interacted with others, and we worried about them. We worried because we know the powerful negative repercussions of isolation.

RESEARCH METHODOLOGY

To tackle this problem directly (and affordably), we secured a grant from AmeriCorps VISTA that provided us with a full-time intern to help explore the problem in depth for 2 years. That first year included a series of focus groups held with affordable housing senior residents—some of which were attended entirely by non-English-speaking residents and were translated. We also conducted focus groups with senior caregivers, service coordinators, and activities coordinators—all people who work directly with seniors daily. The primary questions posed in the focus groups included the following: Do you see certain types of people isolated? Why do you think they (or you) become isolated? What have you tried that was successful in reaching them? What would help you? How can we prevent isolation and its impact in our housing communities?

The discussions and ideas were rich. They showed deep, crucial, and diverse insight into the lives, thoughts, emotions, and behaviors of seniors. To create this book, we combined the concepts generated through the focus groups with academic research and stories as well as with the results of a survey distributed to slightly more than 1,000 senior residents.

The survey was produced in English, Spanish, and Chinese, and answers were analyzed through a number of different systems, including SPSS software for statistical analysis. Although the results weren't entirely unexpected, given what we know through experience, we found that some of the divergences were starker than we anticipated.

We then asked caregivers (while keeping the survey answers confidential) to tell us which of the respondents were socially active and which were socially isolated. We defined *active* as those who visit with at least one other person inside or outside the building at least once a week or are involved in at least one community event or activity. We defined *isolated* as those who do not engage with others or who usually stay in their apartment. The difference between the two groups, as you can see in the charts, is startling.

Active Satellite Seniors report feeling content more often than isolated seniors.

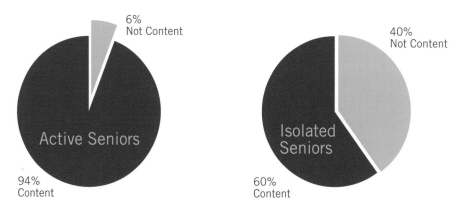

6% Not Content
Active Seniors
94% Content

40% Not Content
Isolated Seniors
60% Content

The conclusion of this project was the self-publication in 2010 of a guide we called *Reach Out! Preventing and Alleviating Social Isolation among Seniors,* which was the precursor to this book. Our goal was to share with our own staff and fellow senior housing providers the insights we had gleaned from our research about the most common causes of social isolation, and then to offer practical suggestions for intervening to help alleviate these problems. Because of the positive response to our guide, we decided to pursue its publication for wider dissemination. *Connecting with Socially Isolated Seniors: A Service Provider's Guide* is the result. It has been updated and expanded to address several additional areas of concern for social isolation and to offer valuable encouragement and advice to the many dedicated professionals who work so diligently and compassionately to help seniors continue to live and thrive independently in their communities.

Social isolation among seniors is incredibly complex in its origins, presentations, and remedies, and it would be impossible to cover in this book every reason it occurs or every way to alleviate it. Isolation can be a huge challenge for staff and families to address because older residents are the most difficult to reach. This book offers a place to start.

Active Satellite Seniors report feeling
hopeful more often than isolated seniors.

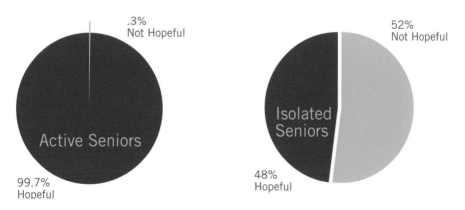

.3%
Not Hopeful

52%
Not Hopeful

Isolated
Seniors

Active Seniors

99.7%
Hopeful

48%
Hopeful

"It makes me feel good to share my life.**"**

—Kit,
Satellite activities
coordinator

1

Introduction

People need one another.

Everyone knows children do not thrive without interaction, but few realize how utterly disabling isolation can be for older adults as well. Elderly adults are becoming our most vulnerable demographic, facing risk factors that include loss of family or friends, being widowed, living alone, having multiple health problems, and confronting rising health care costs.

Consider these three well-known facts:

1. People are living longer.

2. Baby boomers are aging. There are 35 million Americans age 65 or older today, and the U.S. Census Bureau projects a figure of 62 million by 2025—an 80% increase.

3. The cultural norm of "strike out on your own" has resulted in extended families living far away from one another, especially over the last few generations.

The United States is wholly unprepared for the impacts these realities will create. Add them up and it is easy to see why social isolation in seniors is becoming alarmingly widespread and is now recognized as a serious problem. If they are isolated, seniors are less safe; at higher risk of financial, emotional, and physical abuse; and more likely to experience cognitive issues and to decline more rapidly. Seniors at all levels of socioeconomic status experience isolation, but those who live in affordable housing commonly have more risk factors linked with poverty. Simply being poor in America can negatively influence educational opportunities, quality and likelihood of health care access, a family's ability to provide support, and countless other aspects that can

Two residents enjoy making floral arrangements to decorate their holiday parties.

contribute to social isolation. Therefore, those of us who work in affordable senior housing will see even more of this debilitating phenomenon.

Current research demonstrates the harmful effects of isolation and the positive effects of social interaction. A 2007 study conducted by the University of Michigan Institute for Social Research and funded by the National Science Foundation suggests that visiting with a friend or neighbor may be just as helpful in staying *cognitively* sharp as doing a daily crossword puzzle. The researchers found that short-term social interaction lasting for just 10 minutes boosted participants' intellectual performance as much as engaging in so-called "intellectual" activities for the same amount of time.[1] Their findings also suggest that social isolation may negatively affect intellectual abilities as well as emotional well-being. For a society characterized by increasing levels of social isolation, the effects could be far-reaching.

Staff in congregate senior housing see residents who have little to no social interaction as well as residents who might attend some social gatherings but who nevertheless feel lonely, even in the company of a group of neighbors. Both of these types of residents cause concern among service providers in community-based senior housing, and it is for both whom this book is written. One of the many challenges staff face is to be observant of who is in what state, particularly because it can be misleading to assume that a person who seems to be alone must automatically feel lonely. *Social isolation* is the state of being alone and without emotional support systems. *Loneliness* is the feeling of being socially isolated, the unhappy inner perception that one lacks companionship. Having companionship can be as subtle as a senior talking with someone whenever he or she goes to the pharmacy. Take some time to discover all the different aspects of a resident's life that give him or her that necessary connectedness (this can be a slow process, so enjoy it). Reduced social isolation should not be measured exclusively by whether a senior attends all of the building parties. The trick is to learn what each person uniquely needs to reduce any feelings of social isolation.

AGING IN PLACE

Because residents of senior housing want and deserve to "age in place," we, of course, also want them to be able to do so. Most American seniors say they want to stay in their homes for the rest of their lives. In fact, a 2009 AARP survey found this number to be as high as 88% of seniors.[2] As people grow older, they increasingly fear the possibility of having to leave their homes and along with it a comfortable setting and familiar community. Seniors who move into independent affordable living apartments may have lost the home they lived in for years. Others, especially in urban areas, may have rented and were unable to afford market-rate housing after retiring, or they may have moved to the area to be closer to their relatives as they age. There are many reasons why seniors decide to move to affordable housing or other congregate settings. Whatever the cause, the end result is seniors often feel a loss of a certain amount of control, a loss that chips away at their feelings of dignity, quality of life, and independence. Certainly then, seniors have to grapple with leaving the familiar when they move into these types of communities. The service providers and staff who oversee these sites have the great responsibility of understanding and working with the residents from that vantage point. The goal is to provide every opportunity for each senior to develop a new knowledge and sense of home, particularly because he or she may be living there for 20 to 30 years, or longer!

The term *age in place* has become common to many, but nobody wants to just grow as old as possible if they are unhappy. It is time to expand on this important concept and say instead, "Age in place *and* thrive in community." While the focus must be on helping seniors stay in their homes, significant resources and energy must also simultaneously be put into maintaining their quality of life, which is crucial. The goal becomes helping residents feel personally enriched and content *concurrent* with maintaining the ability to age

> "Social isolation and social exclusion are associated with increased rates of premature death and poorer chances of survival after a heart attack. People who get less social and emotional support from others are also more likely to experience lowered feelings of well-being, more depression, and higher levels of disability from chronic diseases.[3]"
>
> —The World Health Organization

in surroundings that feel familiar. This book treats the concepts of aging in place and thriving in community as being inextricably intertwined in preventing and alleviating social isolation among seniors.

Helping seniors do whatever they can to enjoy a good life, regardless of how much money they happen to have, is a worthy mission that includes helping them stay active, connected, and independent for as long as they possibly can be. (In this context, the word *independent* can also mean having adequate supports in place to assist seniors with what they cannot do for themselves.)

The best tool you will ever have is getting to know each resident as the unique human being he or she is. This theme will be repeated often throughout this book because it is a powerful underlying component to providing the best possible care. Of course, you might be providing services for 200 or more residents, so it is not always feasible to expect to get to know every single one. You can, however, work to ensure that each is connected with someone who can provide some semblance of a safety net. With huge caseloads, it is even more important to stay open and flexible, to be a truly active listener, and to gather information constantly throughout your daily interactions and observations with the residents and any family or caregivers with whom you interact. These practices will give you several observational tools:

> **KEY CONCEPT**
>
> The best tool you will ever have is getting to know each resident as the unique human being he or she is.

- A baseline for the residents' typical behaviors, which in turn will allow you to recognize and respond to changes right away

- The opportunity to understand what does light up the residents, what used to light them up, and what might help them light up again or perhaps for the very first time

- A creative approach to problem solving and applying a patchwork of unique solutions for each senior

Truly getting to know people is what allows them to open up. When that happens, it provides the chance to help connect seniors with a cause, person, group, or vision that they can enjoy and see value in. This practice will lead you toward meeting your mission—whether it be your agency's, your own, or both.

Finally, do not forget to enjoy every minute of it. You are providing education, opportunity, and compassion. That is righteous work. All seniors (and all humans!) really just want a good life, right?

We really do need one another.

HOW TO USE THIS BOOK

Sections 2 through 13 discuss the strongest risk factors that lead to social isolation in seniors. Although this is not an all-encompassing list of risks for social isolation, these factors show up repeatedly in the research. Keep in mind, however, that these are generalizations and there will always be people who do not fit the standard norms. At the end of each section is a "How to Help" section to help you address the risks for social isolation. After reading through the various topics covered in this book, you can use the quiz in the Appendix to review your knowledge of social isolation. Finally, the sources cited in the sections can be found in the Notes at the back of the book.

Use the following checklist to help you
begin to identify people with potential
risk factors for becoming socially isolated.

RISK FACTORS CHECKLIST

Physical Health Problems and Disabilities

○ Yes ○ No

If yes, are they multiple, severe, and/or chronic?

○ Yes ○ No

Those with multiple, severe, and/or chronic health problems or disabilities are at more risk than those without many health problems or disabilities.

Substance

○ Yes ○ No

Those who use prescription drugs, street drugs, and/or alcohol in ways that are debilitating are at increased risk for isolation.

Behavioral and Cognitive Health Issues

○ Yes ○ No

Seniors who struggle with behavioral health issues, including hoarding, are at increased risk of isolation, as are those who experience cognitive health problems.

Gender

○ Male ○ Female ○ Transgender

Addressing social isolation presents different challenges for each gender. Those who identify as transgender are at greatest risk, and men are at a higher risk than women.

Lesbian, Gay, or Bisexual

○ Yes ○ No

Seniors who identify as lesbian, gay, or bisexual are at greater risk than those who identify as heterosexual.

Intimate Partnership

○ Single
○ Married
  (or partnered through commitment)
○ Widowed
○ Divorced

Individuals who are single, widowed, separated, or divorced are at greater risk than those who are married or in other long-term, intimate, committed relationships.

Friendships and Pets

○ Yes ○ No

Those without close relationships, such as family, friends, or neighbors with whom they can confide and discuss personal matters, are at greater risk. Those with pets are at reduced risk.

Transportation

○ Yes ○ No

Those who lack access to affordable, accessible, and reliable transportation are at greater risk than those with access.

New to the Area

○ Yes ○ No

Those who are new to the area are at greater risk for becoming socially isolated than those who are familiar with the area.

Language

○ Speaks the more prevalent language in their community?
○ Does not speak the more prevalent language in their community?

Individuals who do not speak the prevalent language (within the individual's building or community) are at greater risk than those who do.

"No amount of money and prestige justifies wasting our precious time, our precious life, doing something that isn't important to us. . . . Fish swim and birds fly; humans work. This is our life and our joy."

—Zoketsu Norman Fischer,
poet and author

2

The Zen of Working with the Socially Isolated

People are terrified of the concept of social isolation. Professionals working with seniors are sometimes less afraid than the general person on the street; many, however, still find it (consciously or subconsciously) one of the more distasteful things to deal with on the job. Why the fear and recoiling, as if social isolation were a highly contagious and probably fatal virus?

Your work is not about avoiding burnout on the job or struggling to stay detached from the issues that residents of community-based housing face. You must be involved, even when it is difficult or uncomfortable. This section offers a way to fully see the hurt in a situation, stay involved, and accept the feelings and challenges that might arise.

For professionals working with seniors, not being able to handle the effects of social isolation on elderly clients can lead, personally, to less peace of mind, a loss of day-to-day contentment in one's work, and a lowered ability to serve those clients. In such cases:

- Some professionals may avoid these clients and/ or their problems, even subconsciously.

- To truly help these clients, professionals need to sincerely demonstrate that they are available to and present for them. If less than sincere, they run the risk of coming across as helpful because "we're doing our job" or helpful because "we feel sorry for you." While these are not necessarily *bad* things, they can tend to distance seniors further and even cause them to feel more alone than before.

So start by taking a few minutes to reflect on how it would feel to be alone in your apartment with no one to call you and chat with you about your day. No one comes by on your birthday. You go out to get groceries sometimes, and maybe someone throws a smile your way, but maybe you are too nervous to smile back. Maybe you wonder why you should get out of bed, and sometimes maybe you do stay in bed except to use the bathroom and eat something. It gets dark outside and you turn on the television. Be there for a minute.

> **KEY CONCEPT**
>
> You really can be with people who are isolated, depressed, and lonely and truly hear what they are going through, yet not experience harm yourself.

I am describing some bleak scenarios, and I want you to really feel how awful they would be for someone. Go ahead and allow yourself to feel socially isolated. But do not be afraid; it will not hurt you to put yourself in these scenarios and spend a few minutes feeling what they are like. Then move out of these scenes in your mind and come back to your day-to-day tasks or just back to reading this book with your professional curiosity. When you do this, you see that you can step into other people's shoes without hurting yourself. You really can be with people who are isolated, depressed, and lonely and truly hear what they are going through, yet not experience harm yourself. It is natural to try avoiding something we feel will do us harm and, of course, it is important that we follow those instincts. But in cases such as interacting with people who are lonely and isolated—maybe sad, maybe depressed—take a closer look at why you shy away from them. Chances are, they represent something you find scary, a situation in which you do not want to ever find yourself or, perhaps, a situation in which you have already found yourself. Just know that that is okay.

You have taken the most important first steps in helping an isolated senior when you have learned how to move beyond intolerance to tolerance, and then on to understanding that, although a situation a senior is facing may not be good, it will not compromise your own life balance to offer help. Even if you get close and listen to piercing stories of pain and loss, it will be okay. You may think it will depress you, and you may be worried that you will mull it over after work. That is okay, too. The old adage of "not taking it home with you" is possible, but often it simply does not happen that way. A situation can be depressing, and the more you try not to think of it, the more you think of it. But if you can get to a place where it does not weigh you down, then you have no reason to worry about whether the issues are "with you" or not after you leave work. So go ahead and think of those tough situations if they arise while you are at home or shopping or picking up your kids. They are not thoughts that need to come with debilitating emotions.

Remind yourself over and over again—and it can take many times before this comes naturally—that part of being human is to experience suffering. Suffering, right along with joy, shows us that we are all interdependent. There are times when we are doing great and times when we are lying flat on our noses in the dust. Most of the time, however, we are just strolling (or stumbling) along, doing the best we can at any given moment.

How to Help

1. Reflect on your attitude from time to time. If you find yourself complaining a lot about work, it might mean you are forgetting that it is yours (i.e., *your* work). The tasks are your responsibility, and if you feel unable to make positive change, forgetting this factor may be why. If you can make changes for the better, then try to. If there are circumstances beyond your control that do not allow you to do so, then there may be other, more subtle things that you can change, such as your approach.

2. Remember to be fully present when you are spending time with a senior. All of your other thoughts will still be there after you finish talking. If you truly focus on the individual senior, you are guaranteed not to have wasted time talking with this unique person.

3. Do something pleasurable every day. Think this through if you do not know right away what that might be. It may not necessarily be something on a standard list of things you are *supposed* to do in order to prevent burnout. It could be something completely outlandish or private, but just pick something that you know gives you at least a few minutes of true happiness.

4. Do at least one thing physically or nutritionally healthy every day. If you are not able to exercise regularly, park farther out in the store parking lot (even if it is raining—breathe in that rain), or eat a raw carrot, or put half a spoon less of sugar in your coffee cup. These little things will remind you that you are strong.

The Zen of Working with the Socially Isolated

5. Stop worrying about how much you are getting done. To-do lists are great, but do not go through them in your mind constantly. They are there so that you can write something down and forget about it until the next time you need to check it. To quote John Lennon, "Life is what happens to you while you're busy making other plans."

6. Be careful that you are not applying your own expectations to people. If one of the seniors with whom you work gets up, reads the newspaper, and listens to talk radio every day—sometimes calling in—you may feel that person is lonely and needs more social connection in his or her life. Perhaps, but first get to know the person well. People certainly need each other on many levels to maximize healthiness and contentment. That particular resident, however, might be quite socially stimulated by what he or she is already doing. After you get to know the person, the two of you might still find additional ways to connect with the world that appeal to him or her. And even if you do not, and if he or she is not lonely, then that is perfectly fine.

7. Have compassion. Have it for all residents, no matter how cranky or dismissive of you they may be. They are just like you in many ways, and very often the crankiness is a result of pain (of the body or of the heart). Have compassion for yourself, too.

" They did not want their friends to see them so helpless or to appear as though they could not care for themselves. **"**

—Satellite resident caregiver

3

Health and
Disabilities

Research has exploded recently on the undeniable correlation between poor health and social isolation. Although we may not know which came first, we do know that being isolated regularly from one's community leads to declining health.[1] The converse is also true: Poor health commonly leads to feelings of isolation; it can be a deeply injurious and often rapid cycle.

Satellite Housing's survey showed that isolated seniors reported health problems at a 12% higher rate than did the overall group. In the focus groups, several service coordinators reported that the residents who frequently participate in activities are the ones without mobility or other major health issues. Health problems can cause physical barriers to making social connections. Even poor vision can make socializing more difficult. As one resident explained, "My trouble is meeting all these new people. I can't see their faces, so I don't recognize them the next time I see them."

In addition to physical barriers, health problems can also lead to emotional distress and depression that hinders social connections. A study of Chicagoans found that the average blood pressure of the least lonely people was 0.6 mm/Hg, lower than others'. This is equal to the effect of statins, the cholesterol-lowering prescription medication.[2] Depression commonly interferes with one's ability to connect with others.

A Chinese caregiver, Pauline, mentioned that she saw many Chinese residents who started to isolate themselves as an illness or disability became more prominent. She explained, "They did not want their friends to see them so helpless or to appear as though they could not care for themselves." If such residents have grown children living nearby, they may allow those children to provide them with help. But if they do not have grown children nearby, these

Sara first caught the attention of service coordinator Katrina after being assessed as a frail resident dealing with macular degeneration and increasing challenges with her activities of daily living. Katrina began visiting Sara often, which allowed them to get to know each other and eventually trust each other. As time went on, Katrina learned of Sara's interest in art and painting and encouraged her to attend the ongoing hobby hour with other residents of the facility where she lived. Sara was reluctant to attend but finally agreed when Katrina assured her that she could simply observe the class if she did not want to participate.

During her first class, Sara sat in the corner watching other residents make jewelry. Iris, the activity leader, noticed her and invited her to join the group. She showed Sara how to make the jewelry, but Sara said she was not interested. Iris continued to work on the jewelry, later suggesting that Sara choose beads that appealed to her. Iris then pulled out some string and threaded the beads with her. Eventually, Sara was making the jewelry by herself, and Iris continued to work closely with her.

The next week, Iris personally invited Sara and walked with her down to hobby hour. "I would go to her room and bring her down just before class," says Iris. "I did that every single week until she eventually got into it and started coming by herself. Now she comes all the time and paints some truly beautiful pieces. It's a matter of not giving up."

Iris then discovered that although Sara enjoyed working on her projects, she did not like getting compliments on her art because, due to her macular degeneration, Sara had a hard time seeing her work. So, rather than praising Sara's art, Katrina and Iris began asking her to tell them about it, which made Sara feel more comfortable. Eventually, as Sara and the other residents started completing more pieces, they wanted a place to showcase their crafts and artwork. The community room was turned into a gallery where residents can now display their work.

Katrina and Iris showed commitment, which helped draw Sara out of social isolation. Their encouragement and understanding of her individuality allowed her to rediscover her interests and talents as an artist and become comfortably involved with her peers once again. Katrina says Sara smiles a lot more these days.

One of Sara's watercolors

KEY CONCEPT

Sometimes self-isolation and confusion can result from the onset of a urinary tract or respiratory infection, a thyroid issue, diabetes, or even a possibly forgotten knock on the head.

residents choose to deal with health issues by themselves.

Incontinence is a common health problem—far more common than most know—that can have a huge impact on women, especially, and lead to social isolation. Often the embarrassment, or just the fear of embarrassment, can be enough to keep women at home, even away from medical appointments. An estimated 25% of women ages 45–64 experience incontinence and the percentage rises to 30% for women age 65 and older, or about 1 in 3 women.[3] This is a health issue that all staff should make a point of helping to bring to the surface for female residents of their community.

Of special note: Sometimes self-isolation and confusion can result from the onset of a urinary tract or respiratory infection, a thyroid issue, diabetes, or even a forgotten knock on the head. If you see changes such as these, especially ones that arise suddenly, remember to consider a possible physical ailment as the source. Work with family members or other support systems to get the resident to a doctor as soon as possible, because these types of conditions are treatable and the person can usually return to a normal, active life in a short time. If left untreated, however, these conditions can quickly become more serious, possibly even leading to delirium, which is dangerous and difficult to treat. (See Section 4, Alzheimer's Disease and Cognitive Health, for more information on these health challenges.)

1. Because health and isolation are so tightly linked, make it a priority to keep track of residents' activities of daily living (ADL) limitations and work with them to find ways to manage these limitations. This is best done in tandem with their health care practitioners by setting up appropriate in-home care, reasonable accommodations, or physical therapy, or by procuring assistive devices such as a rocking knife (for food preparation) or a walker.

2. Home visits are great and should be done often for those who are frail. In between visits and office discussions, you can also simply pay attention when you see frail residents walking through the lobby or attending an event. Note the steadiness of their gait, their level of grooming, or whatever aspect might be improving or declining. Regular check-ins are an opportunity for you and residents to connect more deeply, and they give you a chance to learn something new about each resident's unique life. The monitoring itself is an effective tool against isolation when done with sincere interest. For example, you do not need to ask merely, "How is your eating going, Mr. Ting?" Instead, you might know that Mr. Ting loves birds and you can also ask him with a smile, "Have you seen any hummingbirds this morning?" Mr. Ting will likely feel good about the personal question, and during the interaction, you can observe whether he looks thinner or dehydrated, or has less energy.

3. Become thoroughly knowledgeable about your local in-home support services programs and help residents through the application process where needed. Connect with at least one staff person at the program who you know to be responsive.

Health and Disabilities

4. When talking with residents, regardless of their health status, remember to ask them once in a while whether they have seen their doctor recently. If they have not, offer to help set up an appointment. Work with them to overcome any obstacles to appointments, such as transportation, fear, or language barriers.

5. Work with your local clinics or hospitals to bring in a public health nurse who is accustomed to working with seniors, bimonthly or more frequently. The nurse may be able to perform basic health screening procedures, such as checking blood pressure and blood sugar levels.

6. When you see a more abrupt withdrawal, enlist the help of a family member or other support person to get the resident to a doctor quickly. In general, never hesitate to call residents' health care practitioners with concerns or worrisome observations about their health. (Of course, if it is a matter they disclosed to you privately, you will need a signed release of information.)

7. Bring in a public health nurse or a health educator to hold a group meeting to discuss ways to address the problem of urinary incontinence. Be sure the presenter talks about pelvic floor exercises, called Kegels, that women can do to abate the issue. Then you can post signs here and there that say something like "remember to do 3 Kegels today!"

"This is the best thing that has ever happened to me. I've been able to focus on me and my memories of my life. Thank you for helping me remember me."

—Odessa, Satellite resident

4

Alzheimer's Disease and Cognitive Health

If you work with seniors, you have certainly heard many of them fret about forgetfulness. A bit of this is normal, because age-related changes related to memory and cognition are seen in most older adults, including the following:

- It takes longer to process information.

- Short-term memory declines (e.g., people's names or recent events are less easily recalled).

- Some older adults may experience small declines in problem-solving abilities.

> ## KEY CONCEPT
>
> Caregivers can be crucial in recognizing the possible early onset of Alzheimer's disease and promptly bringing in support systems.

One researcher has noted that "most people over 65 experience a level of forgetfulness that is merely inconvenient and generally involves typically unimportant information."[1] Social isolation, however, can be a red flag for a more serious decline in memory and cognition. Loss of interest in or withdrawal from normal activities can be symptoms of early Alzheimer's disease or dementia. They can also be warning signs for possible depression, substance abuse, or other problems. Social isolation is not exclusive to individuals with Alzheimer's disease. The possibility, however, should be considered, especially when social isolation is combined with changes in basic self-care abilities (dressing, bathing, toileting, eating), forgetting the names of everyday objects (pen, knife, table), changes in the ability to complete routine daily activities (shopping, preparing food, putting dishes away properly), or losing one's way on

STAYING SOCIALLY CONNECTED MAY
HELP PREVENT ALZHEIMER'S DISEASE.

Researchers from the Rush Center studied 823 people with an average age of 80, none of whom had dementia at the start of the study. Over a 4-year period, researchers asked the participants about their social activity—whether they felt they had enough friends and whether they felt abandoned or experienced a sense of emptiness. Over the 4 years, 76 people in the study developed Alzheimer's disease. Those who did were more likely to have poor social networks.[2]

STAYING CALM AND CONNECTED MAY
REDUCE THE RISK OF DEVELOPING DEMENTIA.

Researchers who published their findings in the *Journal of Neurology* asked 500 healthy people over age 70 to fill out questionnaires about their personalities. Those who were calm and relaxed had a 50% lower risk of developing dementia compared to people who were socially isolated and prone to distress during the 6 years of the study.[3]

a familiar path. These changes can indicate more serious changes that need further investigation and consultation with a professional. Caregivers can be crucial in recognizing the possible early onset of Alzheimer's disease and promptly bringing in support systems.

Many older people can also experience cognitive changes and decline due to reversible factors such as poor nutrition, untreated infections (urinary tract infection, severe gum disease), the interaction effects of different medications, lack of proper sleep, or emotional disturbances. The latter

66The generally accepted knowledge about the brain is that it starts going downhill fairly early in life, which is true, and that there is little one can do about changing that pattern, which is not true. Increases in cortical growth as a consequence of stimulating environmental input have been demonstrated at every age, including very old age.[5] **99**

—Dr. Marian Diamond, Professor of Integrative Biology, University of California Berkeley

can include anxiety or depression, substance use or abuse, or major grief or loss.

For isolated seniors, these treatable causes of cognitive decline can worsen if no one is paying attention or marking such changes. Caregivers need to pay attention to these types of changes and not assume they are normal or will pass without immediate and proper interventions. If changes are noted, those affected should be encouraged to see their doctor to investigate the potential causes and possible treatments.

Another invaluable aspect of service coordination is providing or finding opportunities for residents to participate in activities associated with delaying the onset of cognitive decline. Recent research demonstrates persuasively that good nutrition, stress reduction, physical exercise, and learning new things might effectively stave off cognitive decline. Social interaction in and of itself commonly can improve cognitive abilities as people exercise the muscle that is their brain.

It is never too late (and never too soon!) to start these practices. As Dr. Susanne Sorensen, head of research at the British Alzheimer's Society, states, "Compelling new evidence suggests people who are easily stressed or not very outgoing should make every effort to be socially active."[4] People earn the greatest protection against cognitive decline when they remain engaged in activities involving multiple tasks that require communication, interaction, and organization; continued learning; and constant challenges for their brains.[4]

How to Help

1. Always seek new ways to provide a stimulating environment for your residents:

- New workshops on music, languages, or other skills
- Technology equipment, where possible
- Word games, riddles, and puzzles
- Opportunities for diverse forms of creative expression

2. Emphasize activities that include opportunities for social interaction. Even at a Fourth of July barbecue held at your building you can add a simple game that involves some way to make fun connections. For example, give out a prize to the person who finds someone with the birthday nearest his or her own.

3. Suggest that residents bring pictures, mementos, or stories to a coffee hour and talk about them. This can be a powerful way to stimulate memory and make connections with others at the same time.

4. Develop a library of donated books. Many people will be happy to give you their old ones. Work with a willing resident to become the librarian and oversee the checkout process. Facilitate the start of a book club or a chapter club.

5. Schedule exercise classes in which anyone can participate. You can bring in skilled volunteers to lead anything from a very gentle chair exercise to a group walk around the park. (An aside on volunteers: Running an effective and safe volunteer pool can be a big project! There are many volunteer match agencies that can provide training and guidance in how to best go about this endeavor.)

Alzheimer's Disease and Cognitive Health

6. Healthy eating is one of the pillars of brain health, so offer regular workshops on nutrition. Find easy-to-prepare recipes for your newsletter. If a Brown Bag or other free grocery program is available in your area, help make it accessible to the residents. Ask residents periodically whether they have been eating well.

7. Pay attention to signs of possible cognitive decline; they may signal an underlying physical health issue or may be an early indicator of dementia. Residents should feel comfortable coming to you with their worries about this form of decline, and you should feel comfortable talking with them about any significant changes you have noticed.

8. Help worried residents or their families prepare a list of concerns ahead of time to bring to their primary care practitioners.

9. Provide contact information for helpful resources. The Alzheimer's Association is a fabulous national resource for any Alzheimer's-related services (1-800-272-3900; http://www.alz.org). Another resource to provide to the family is Caregiver Resource Centers (1-800-445-8106; http:// www.caregiver.org).

66 I think people who are depressed are sometimes actually mad as hell but too polite to say so. **99**

—Dorothy,
Satellite administrator

5

Emotional
Health

Struggles with emotional health issues can affect any age group or demographic. Emotional or mental health is how we think, feel, and act as we manage our daily lives; it influences how we deal with stress, relate to others, and make choices. When layered with risk factors related to seniors, struggles with emotional health can have a disproportionately high co-occurrence with isolation. Some seniors experience tremendous loss, which can make them highly susceptible to depression. In fact, older people account for 20% of all suicide deaths in the United States— the highest rates of any age group.[1] Yet the emotional health needs of seniors are some of the most underserved.

KEY CONCEPT

Older people account for 20% of all suicide deaths in the United States—the highest rates of any age group. Yet the emotional health needs of seniors are some of the most underserved.

The American Geriatrics Society attributes these surprising facts to seniors' being more likely to see a general practitioner, who is less likely to identify and treat a behavioral health need than would a mental health practitioner.[2] Additionally, many seniors grew up in a time of less public awareness and understanding of mental health issues. Thus they may hesitate to admit, even to themselves, that there might be a problem or to seek help.

Depression can lead to social isolation as well as stem from it. A lack of general social support is a key factor in many people's depression. Keeping people connected is, therefore, rather important in preventing depression and helping to resolve it.

Some symptoms of depression that are not associated with normal grief include an intense and pervasive sense of guilt, thoughts of suicide or a preoccupation with dying (especially if making concrete plans), slow speech and body movements, inability to perform activities of daily living, seeing or hearing things that are not real, and feelings of hopelessness and helplessness. Other warning signs, which may also be a part of a normal grieving process unless combined with the symptoms previously listed, can include excessive sadness or crying, loss of appetite, excessive sleeping, and loss of interest in things once cared about.

Depression not only makes someone *feel* sick—with aches, pains, and fatigue—but also actually worsens physical health and may interfere with memory and concentration. Be aware, however, that several medical problems can also contribute to depression-like symptoms. These problems, which need to be examined by a knowledgeable geriatrician to distinguish them from true depression, include Parkinson's disease, stroke, heart disease, cancer, diabetes, thyroid disorders, vitamin B_{12} deficiency, dementia, lupus, and multiple sclerosis. Depression-like behaviors can also result from the interaction effects of certain medications. The first line of response to symptoms of depression in an older adult is for him or her to have a thorough physical examination to rule out other causes.

If a person is truly experiencing depression, many treatments have been found to be effective, including psychotherapy, support groups, brief behavioral–cognitive therapy, and medications (which must be carefully calibrated and monitored by a professional—especially if a person is already taking other medications).

EDDIE'S STORY

Eddie kept to himself, never joining in any of the activities that happened on-site, and only occasionally was he seen leaving the building. He was affable enough—always returning a brief smile if someone greeted him—but no matter how many different ways the service coordinator tried to engage him, he never stopped to talk. He still drove and had his own car, so he never even needed to ride the bus for group grocery shopping trips (which can encourage social connections).

The community activities coordinator started a storytelling group at Eddie's building, and to everyone's amazement, Eddie came. He said later he had been walking by the community room and heard a story and was drawn in. After a few sessions, Eddie somewhat awkwardly started putting together brief stories when it was his turn. Although the group leader strongly encouraged everyone to tell a story about themselves, Eddie did not. But he did start recounting more and more about people he had known and became more comfortable talking. After a few months, one of the other participants told a story about how her son had gone to jail; she went on to say how proud she was of him because he had turned his life around when he got out.

Eddie was moved by this story. The next week, he surprised everyone by telling a very personal story about himself. He told his story eloquently and with deep regret, and the listeners were moved by it. It turned out he had spent 40 years off and on in prison for robbery and murder and was ashamed. He had been depressed for years—sometimes, he said, too depressed to eat.

Eddie commented on how relieved he was that no one in the group had shown the slightest bit of judgment and instead had prompted him by asking questions because they were interested in his history. It was clearly a pivotal experience for him. Eddie said there was a guy who had been trying to get him to come to a Narcotics Anonymous group forever and he never would go because, as he put it, "I have no social skills; I've been in the pen most of my life." But after opening up in the storytelling group, he decided he could give NA a try. He is now in his third year of being clean and goes to NA every single day.

Eddie says he still does not have a lot of friends, but that he has a few, and that he did not have any when he first moved into the community. Telling his story seems to have liberated him. He now connects well with other members of the group.

POSITIVE AGING

The view that aging is all about continuous decline can be countered with the concept of *positive aging*. More than preventing decline and illness, positive aging involves maintaining or improving health and well-being as seniors age. This does not mean that seniors need to be cheery and bubbly all the time. Of course, real life is made up of a full range of self-aware emotions, and seniors might naturally run into health problems. As noted by Jaquelyn Browne, head of the Fischler School of Education and Human Services at Nova Southeastern University: "Positive aging is a way to highlight that there are both gains as well as losses in aging, and it is time to focus on the gains."[3]

How to Help

1. For residents who have many supports available, but who still cannot seem to break out of their shells, think of mental health as a possible underlying (or overriding) problem. You will find that many seniors will not want to talk about this subject in reference to themselves. You can help them address their emotional/behavioral needs without using clinical language. It is far more effective to discuss what is keeping them from feeling healthy or happy or what is making them anxious than it is to use words such as *disorder* or *mental illness*.

2. Because primary care practitioners are less likely to recognize or treat a mental health issue, recommend behavioral health services to residents in addition to their regular doctor.

Emotional Health

3. Make sure residents have access to their local or national suicide hotline phone numbers (1-800-784-2433 [or 1-800-SUICIDE]; 1-800-273-8255 [1-800-273-TALK]; or TTY: 1-800-799-4889). Often, people may not want to pick up the phone and tell someone they are thinking of killing themselves. A very powerful tool is a resource that goes by the name of a "friendship line" or a "warmline" instead of a hotline. With these resources, a senior can call someone caring and supportive to talk with without the attached stigma of admitting his or her own suicidal feelings. Seek out centers for elderly suicide prevention. They are rare but exist. See the Institute on Aging's Center for Elderly Suicide Prevention website for words of wisdom (http://www.ioaging.org/services/cesp_suicide_prevention_help.html).

"Being high is such an effective pain-number; you have to learn to understand it's OK to feel pain again, because you will."

—Satellite resident

6

Substance Use

As discussed earlier, a significant amount of loss typically accompanies aging (e.g., loss of a partner, family, independence, physical abilities). Not only does loss make one susceptible to depression, but it also raises the risk of vulnerability to the misuse of alcohol or drugs or to the overuse of prescription medications. In fact, seniors are at a higher risk for alcoholism in reaction to life stressors than is any other age group.[1]

And the situation is not getting any better: Prevalence rates of alcohol abuse and dependence in older adults are likely to increase as baby boomers—who have heavier drinking habits than the previous cohort of older adults— reach older age.[2]

It is estimated that the number of adults age 50 or older with alcohol or drug-related problems will double from an annual average of 2.8 million from 2002–2006 to 5.7 million in 2020. This group's nonmedical use of prescription psychotropic drugs, in particular, is predicted to grow as well.[3]

This aspect of working with seniors can be complex for both nonclinical and clinical service providers. The same common signs and symptoms displayed with substance abuse can also be connected to depression, cognitive decline, or a combination of two or more of the factors listed below. Many substance abuse treatment centers provide the following list of warning signs that may indicate an alcohol- or medication-related problem in older adults:

KEY CONCEPT

Substance abuse is a serious problem that creates a high risk of falls and suicide in seniors, compounded by a decreased motivation to ask for help.

- Being unsure of oneself

- Irritability, sadness, or depression

- Unexplained chronic pain

- Isolation

- Difficulty staying in touch with family or friends

- Lack of interest in usual activities

Some medications can cause side effects that influence a person's mental state, and some may interact in such a way as to cause depression or anxiety. Furthermore, certain prescriptions may not mix well with over-the-counter medications. Self-medicating or experiencing inadequate doctor–patient communication can also lead to complications.

Talk about confusing! It may even be confusing to seniors themselves in that they may not be aware of any complications associated with their prescription medications. People in their support systems may even encourage misuse inadvertently because they want to help seniors decrease their pain.

Do not hide your concern for residents, but also assure them that they, not you, make the choices in their lives and that the choices they make will not affect your personal opinions of them (and sincerely stick with this!). Then make sure they know all the options they have for change—from getting completely clean to cutting back substance expenses by $10 a month or by one drink a week—any option that makes sense to them. Your job is to help them reduce the harm that comes with using. If they decide to start using only at night, or only with a friend, then that is a great step, and you can encourage and support it. Sometimes a first step

MARTY'S STORY

Marty has struggled with severe alcoholism for over 40 years, and he calls himself an alcoholic. A service coordinator who knew he sang at the Fat Lady Bar in Oakland for decades asked him to sing at some of the Thanksgiving and winter parties at a couple of other senior communities. The coordinator told Marty he would not be allowed to do the performances if he was drinking, because of the safety risks. Marty said he would sober up, and he did so by the end of October. After the holiday season ended, however, he started drinking again. Each year since then he has stayed sober for about two and a half months in the autumn in order to do these performances. Today he tells us he has been sober for several months.

Marty is aware of all of his options for recovery and for reducing the harmful effects of drinking. Because he trusts the service coordinator not to harangue him, he is able to talk freely with her and learn of all his options. He occasionally contemplates the idea of going into rehab, and we hope one day he will. For now, however, he has made a plan with the service coordinator to drink water several times throughout the day to avoid dehydration. He also goes to a group across the street where he can be open and real with other people who have been through the same thing. He sees some of his neighbors from his building at the group and, while he doesn't discuss drinking with them when he sees them in the halls, he says it makes them all feel more neighborly.

Staying sober is no small feat for Marty, but even during the months when he is, it is certainly more positive for his overall health than drinking year round. He also says he is saving money. Although the service coordinator is concerned about Marty, she is also impressed with what he has been able to do for himself as well as others.

might even be when they agree that, yes, substance abuse does cause problems. And this step may be all that happens for several months at a time. The second step might be that they agree to increase their water intake, which can reduce the health risks of dehydration that commonly accompany alcohol use. Go with it—while always making yourself as available as you can be for support.

These scenarios lead back to your most useful tool: knowing the senior. Establishing early trust and communication with seniors will help you know what is going on in their lives and can help you sort through the possible issues. Substance abuse is a serious problem that *creates a high risk of falls and suicide in seniors, compounded by a decreased motivation to ask for help.* You may be tempted to think "Well, he's 69 . . . why should he stop drinking now?" But if he had diabetes, you would not say "Well, he might as well eat lots of sugary foods since he's 69." Both are diseases that will cause organ and other health issues and lead to an early death. Whether someone has 1 year or 30 years left to live, each day deserves to be spent with as much health and contentment as possible.

1. Choose your words carefully. You need to show that you accept the senior not just as someone with needs, but also as *someone*.

2. There is never any need to use the words *alcoholic*, *alcoholism*, or *addiction* unless a senior chooses to use them. The behaviors are what cause problems for the person, so the behaviors are what you need to talk about (and "talk" mostly means "listen"). Collaboratively discuss the problems drinking and using cause for the individual, and work on ways to tackle those issues as the senior feels ready.

3. As seniors cut back, help them have something to replace the dependency, such as taking care of a pet, attending support groups, volunteering, or engaging in prayer or meditation.

4. Seniors may not be sure whether their doctors know all the medications they are using. Sometimes, seniors see a few different doctors. Help them make lists of all the prescription drugs they use and encourage them to take the list to one primary doctor to discuss.

Substance Use

5. Remember that the only people who can reduce substance use are the users themselves.

6. Work with individuals closely to get to their health care practitioner if you observe warning signs of substance abuse along with signs of possible cognitive changes, differences in eating habits, or trouble with physical coordination. If you feel the need is urgent—especially if an individual's behavior is observed publicly—inform the health care provider of the situation if the person refuses to go to his or her provider.

7. The next time you organize a health or wellness event, provide information about over-the-counter (OTC) and prescription medication misuse. Encourage residents to keep an up-to-date list of all medications (prescription, OTC, and vitamin and herbal supplements). Make or find a form to distribute to residents that lists medications and dosage information.

8. *Remember:* These people are survivors. They have a lot of strengths.

"When in doubt,
throw it out.**"**

—My mom

7

Hoarding

The urge to accumulate is powerful. Most of us have felt it to some degree. It is when it gets out of control that it starts negatively affecting quality of life and can get pretty hazardous—especially to a senior. When a resident accumulates a cumbersome amount of personal belongings (not just a collection), recognize it as a complex need for help.

The term *hoarding* used to be unfamiliar to most people, even those who hoarded possessions. But now, thanks to reality television, the term is commonly used and understood. Television shows the most extreme cases, but there are thousands of other individuals who have less sensational stories and who struggle every day. Obviously, the chances of falling are high when a home has huge stacks of newspapers, several appliances that do not work, or piles of clothes. A senior's self-care diminishes as the bathroom or kitchen gets too full of possessions to navigate. And, yes, people can experience increased isolation as a result of hoarding, because they do not want others to see their mess.

More commonly, hoarding is a *result* of loneliness. Some clinicians believe that "hoarding increases among older adults as compensation for accumulated human losses."[1] In other words, stuff replaces relationships.

Mark Salazar, program manager at the Mental Health Association of San Francisco, notes that the onset of hoarding typically happens at a younger age and grows worse as a person ages, with more than 50% of those who hoard intensely being age 60 or older. They may feel as if objects are more reliable than people and that they can trust things better than people.[2]

Hoarding can come in the form of compulsive buying, picking up all free items regardless of their value, applying sentimental or aesthetic value to objects, accumulating with an intention to sell the items to increase income, and so forth.

Some seniors see it as thrifty and insist that each object may be useful one day. Regardless of what form hoarding takes, the common factor is extreme distress at the thought of parting with any accumulated items.

> **KEY CONCEPT**
>
> More commonly, hoarding is a result of loneliness. In other words, stuff replaces relationships.

Many seniors do not consciously or subconsciously recognize hoarding as a negative issue in their lives. Behavioral theorists have many hypotheses about the origin of hoarding behavior, including that it is closely related to anxiety disorder (especially social anxiety), as well as proceeding from socialization, response to trauma, or comorbidity with attention deficit–hyperactivity disorder. What we do know is that up to one third of people with serious hoarding problems also experience major depression.[3]

Regardless of how it is classified, hoarding shows up at some level in nearly every residential community. It is incredibly tough to resolve, so it is important to have information about how to approach it.

Consider the suggestions in the "How to Help" section. Remember to underscore anything you do with gentleness and patience. You do not have to launch a campaign for hoarding residents to get rid of everything, unless they express that it is truly their goal. In fact, eliminating all hoarding is almost always the wrong technique. You can help seniors find ways to keep items but to organize them so that they still have full use of their rooms, whenever possible. You can help them start paring down gradually by ending just a single magazine subscription or sorting gradually over time. Talk with each person first to find out what the individual's story is and what the unique advantages and disadvantages are for that person in acquiring and holding on to things.

1. If you think individuals have a problem with hoarding, refrain from devaluing their possessions by calling it "junk." Understand that their things are meaningful to them. Always express empathy and validate the fact that they likely have mixed feelings about whether or how they tackle the hurdle. Also, know that there will almost always be resistance or that, if progress is made, there will be setbacks. Stay patient and flow with it—hoarding is a tough one.

2. Help seniors give objects new meaning and purpose through donations to people who have less than they have.

3. Resources are available through community mental health centers if the situation becomes a health risk or if the resident faces eviction.

4. Find out whether there are peer or clinical groups or treatment in your area specifically for reducing hoarding and cluttering. The Mental Health Association of San Francisco has many resources on their website about hoarding and cluttering (http://www.mha-sf.org/). They also recommend programs that involve various types of groups and, quite significantly, an empathetic peer-coaching match, which might just be the most effective method of all.

Hoarding

5. Help launch peer groups for people who want support cutting back on their hoarding.

6. Help residents by working with them on a long-range plan, beginning with something small such as choosing a time (just before brushing teeth or at lunch), to sort through any new mail that has arrived that day. Another time could be when they take off an item of clothing; they either put it in their laundry basket, in a drawer, or hang it up. Work with them to make this a habit before tackling a second rule. Be sure to make each habit something that they have suggested or chosen from a list and one that they feel they can do.

7. A must-read is *Compulsive Hoarding and Acquiring* by Gail Steketee and Randy O. Frost (Oxford University Press, 2007). It has an accompanying workbook that you can use to help residents examine their discomfort level with getting rid of possessions and their triggers for getting more. It offers tips and tools for filing, sorting, and organizing to help people manage their clutter.

"Do not depend only
on your husband.
He is not immortal.**"**

—Aiying,
Satellite resident

8

Intimate Partnerships

First, some notes on the terms used in this section:

- The word *marriage* refers to any type of adult, committed, intimate relationship, regardless of the gender of the individuals involved.

- The pronoun *he* appears frequently in this section because among the generations we serve, usually it was the man who relied on the woman to do most of the domestic tasks, such as cooking, cleaning, and arranging social events. In these modern times, it may be difficult to feel sympathy for a situation that could now be perceived as sexist. But understand that it was simply the cultural norm for a time in this country and still is in many families.

> 66 Loneliness is the perception of being alone and can be experienced even when one is in contact with others. Although older persons can live alone without being socially isolated or feeling lonely, living alone is a leading indicator of the potential for social isolation.[1] 99

Approximately 63% of the residents in Satellite Housing communities live without a significant other. Those who are married but do not have a circle of friends are at a very high risk of suffering from the ill effects associated with isolation when they lose their spouse or significant other. Widowhood commonly creates a loss of the emotional support that may not have been recognized until it was gone. Losing one's spouse can also mean a loss of instrumental support. If the other spouse was the homemaker, the responsibilities for maintaining the household then fall on the surviving partner, and these responsibilities can be daunting to the point where he may start to feel overwhelmed and withdrawn. He must now prepare the meals, do the cleaning, and maintain the budget, among other important tasks.

Couples who self-identify as lesbian, gay, bisexual, or transgendered (LGBT) face additional challenges as they age and lose their partners. Seniors aged 65 and older were raised in an era during which discrimination against gay and lesbian individuals was everywhere. LGBT residents may think they need to hide their grief, which of course puts them at high risk for depression and loneliness. It is therefore especially important that LGBT residents living in residential settings (an average of 1 out of every 10 residents) develop ways to cope with neighbors who may still retain those negative attitudes.

> "All of the older sexual minorities groups are less likely to be partnered or married, which likely reflects limited access to marriage and may result in less support as they age. Older gay and bisexual men, compared to older heterosexual men, have significantly fewer children in the household and are significantly more likely to live alone.[2]"

In 2009, the Department of Housing and Urban Development (HUD) announced the explicit ban on discrimination against the LGBT population in subsidized rentals and public housing, which is a significant step in protecting LGBT seniors in the hundreds of thousands of HUD–subsidized elderly housing sites across the country.[3]

RISK OF SUICIDE

Risk of suicide also becomes a factor after the loss of an intimate partner. Following the death of a spouse or partner, if you hear a resident say something like "I want to die too so I can be with her," it is very important to explore that statement further. A natural reaction might be: "Mr. Corea, you'll feel better soon," but that translates as telling him that he should pull himself together emotionally at a time when that might feel impossible. A much more useful reaction

GARY'S STORY

Gary Wilson has a wonderful sense of humor and laughed when he told me how he first met his partner, Ricardo: "I went to a cheap movie about tigers. And there was a man there who looked at me and I looked at him, and so afterwards we talked in the lobby and then eventually started dating." Gary says Ricardo is the kindest, most honest and trustworthy person he has ever known.

In 2007, Gary realized he needed to move. He had to get rid of his car because he could no longer see well enough to drive, and he could not keep up with the rent at the mobile home park where he was living. He eventually moved into affordable housing. Ricardo also could not afford to stay in the city and moved to Texas where his family had some land. Even though they stay in touch by phone, Gary says it was "horrible" when Ricardo left and that he misses him on so many levels, even to the point of simply having someone he knew he could depend on to help him with the basic stuff. When his printer died, he said to himself "Dangit, Ricardo—I need you here to help me get this printer to the dump!"

The only way Gary got through the loss was spending time on his dog and talking to good friends. He shared with me some very wise words: "If people build and self-contain their life around just one person, then when that person is gone, for whatever reason, they have nothing." He says he learned this the hard way. Gary comes from a huge extended family in the South Bay area, and when they found out he was gay, he lost them all, even to the point where they ordered him to stay out of their county. He had to build a new support network from scratch and did so person by person. He says it is hard work, but that you have to do it. Get involved in a church near you, or volunteer at a library. Gary attends a Lutheran church a block from his apartment where he is warmly welcomed and helps cook breakfast for homeless youth. He says to get involved *before* the pain hits. If not, do it *through* your pain, such as going to a grief support group or asking someone to take a walk with you.

Gary counts his blessings and always stays positive. He joked near the end of our conversation: "Ricardo asks me sometimes if I have a new boyfriend. I tell him 'look, it's like a dog chasing a car—what in the world would the dog do with it if he ever actually caught it?'"

Warning signs of suicidality in older adults[3]:

- Statements of hopelessness or helplessness (e.g., "I don't know if I can go on")

- Disruption of sleep patterns

- Increased alcohol or prescription drug use

- Failure to take care of oneself or to follow medical orders

- Stockpiling medications

- Sudden interest in firearms

- Social withdrawal or elaborate good-byes

- Rush to complete or revise a will

- Overt suicide threats

would be: "Mr. Corea, you sound so sad. Do you really want to die?" Listen carefully to the answer. If it is something along the lines of "Oh no, of course not. I just miss her so much" or "You wouldn't believe how much it hurts," then talk more and listen well. Later, as the conversation wraps up, strongly encourage him to see his doctor to talk about his feelings, and help him arrange the doctor visit, because grief can be paralyzing. Check in often, and keep an eye on his levels of support and recovery.

If his answer to your initial question sounds more like "Well, I know I'll never be happy again. I have nothing to live for. I could easily die and no one would miss me," then that shows a high risk of suicide—especially if he has thoughts of the method he will use. Tell him that you are worried about him and want him to talk with a doctor right away. If he resists your urging, let him know that you are going to bring in a mobile crisis team because you want him to live.

How to Help

1. Encourage married residents with few other social supports to become more involved in other types of activities and groups both within the building and in the larger community. Helping residents enlarge their social map is a good idea in general, but in this instance, it is also a preventive measure in case of the loss of their partners.

2. Those in the early phase of adjustment to loss are at the most risk for becoming socially isolated. Poor adjustment may require increased support, commonly related to household chores. Check in often. If residents whose spouses or partners have recently died complain of sleeplessness or lack of appetite, or appear to be neglecting themselves, work with them to connect with their doctors. Watch for signs of suicidality. Do a new ADL/IADL (instrumental activities of daily living) functional assessment a few months after the death of a partner.

3. Seek out other grief and loss support groups in the community. Many hospitals offer these, and some may be tailored for LGBT (lesbian, gay, bisexual, and transgender) communities. Some residents may prefer to share their deepest feelings with people they do not live near. There are various resources that provide telephone support, social potlucks, companion visitors, and other services for LGBT seniors. Another helpful organization is the national resource center SAGE (Services and Advocacy for Gay, Lesbian, Bisexual, and Transgender Elders; http://www.sageusa.org).

Intimate Partnerships

4. Wherever possible, facilitate the launch of a peer support group dealing with grief and loss.

5. Some people who encounter grieving individuals ask how they are doing only to be polite or because they do not know what else to say. Be sure to let your grieving residents know that you truly care and that you want to know how they really are doing. Ask open-ended questions such as "What kind of day are you having?" Avoid making comments such as "You poor thing."

6. Come up with a buddy system in your building. That way, if a resident does experience the death of a spouse or intimate partner and does not have a circle of friends, there is at least one person on the floor or in the building who will check in on him or her.

7. If the surviving resident wishes, help him or her hold a small memorial at the property. It can feel very supportive to have just a picture with a candle and a card that everyone can sign and give to the bereaved resident.

8. Make sure everyone has access to their local or national suicide hotline phone numbers. See the How to Help section in Section 5 for more information.

"Being feminine or masculine is about being able to be ourselves and being able to laugh at ourselves.**"**

—Enrique,
Satellite property manager

9

Gender

Approximately 80% of the nine million seniors living alone in the United States are women.[1] This figure is linked, of course, to the fact that the life expectancy of women exceeds that of men. The gap between male and female life expectancy is 4.9 years.[2] Add to that the fact that in 2010 the median age at first marriage for women was 26 and for men 29.[3] The mathematical result is that most women who marry men can expect to live almost 6 years as widows.[4] Ironically, though, social isolation is more frequent in men than in women.

Women tend to disproportionately experience hardships related to the death of a spouse or partner, access to transportation, financial struggles, and safety concerns; men, however, experience a greater risk of loneliness.[5] Whereas women represent a greater percentage of seniors who live alone, men experience social isolation at much higher rates. Men are less likely to experience the death of a spouse. Therefore, if a man does experience the loss of his significant other, the results may be more harmful.

In the eras when today's seniors generally married, men typically acted as the stoic counterparts to what they deemed to be women's "more emotional" demeanor. If a man becomes depressed, it can be extremely difficult to pinpoint because men (especially older men) are less likely to admit to the distress, even to themselves. This frequently means these men will be less willing than women to ask for help. A November 2011 posting to John Hopkins Medicine's Healthy Living Alerts discussed this issue:

> Many men find it difficult to discuss their emotions, sexual difficulties, relationship problems, mental health issues like stress and depression, or physical problems—especially those that affect urination, defecation, or intercourse. They simply have not been "programmed" to talk about these things, and

they aren't used to doing so. As a result, men may delay or avoid doctor visits, even (or especially) when they suspect something is wrong."[6]

Loneliness is another one of those out-of-bound topics for men and puts them at a higher risk for the negative health effects that can accompany depression or prolonged solitude. Of every 100,000 people ages 65 and older, 14 died by suicide in 2007. This figure is higher than the national average of 11 suicides per 100,000 people in the general population.[7] White men age 85 or older had an even higher rate, with 47 suicide deaths per 100,000.[8]

Researchers who noted the disparity in suicide rates between Hispanics and non-Hispanic whites have said that *familism*—an emphasis on close relationships with extended kinship—may offer Hispanics better protection against suicide. Experts say that, in general, Hispanics tend to maintain closer relationships with family members than do whites.[9]

Residents celebrate the opening of their community garden.

ROBERT'S STORY

When 90-year-old Robert first heard about a new program that matched seniors as reading partners with at-risk preschoolers, he was excited about the prospect. Even though he had never done this kind of work before, the thought of it delighted him and he joined immediately.

From the first session, he appeared to thrive and truly enjoy it, missing only one session. He built relationships with other seniors involved in the program and engaged in lively conversations with them during breaks. He told Asha, the activities coordinator, that the weekly routine and the good feeling of volunteering with children made him feel confident. He said none of the other available volunteer opportunities had ever appealed to him.

The program, however, lasted only a year. Soon after it ended, staff were surprised to see Robert visibly withdrawing from other people in the building. He stopped participating in the other social activities he had participated in regularly. His interaction with staff also declined, and when he did talk with them, he seemed distant. The program appeared to have acted as a social tonic, providing, as he himself had said, an overall confidence that affected other parts of his life.

Unable to connect with Robert anymore, Asha met with the on-site caregiver, Katrina, about ways to re-engage him. Asha also contacted other seniors from the program, asking if they would reach out to him. She thought that, as his peers, they might be able to reach Robert, but nothing brought him back out of his shell. Finally, Asha spoke with the staff at a nearby elementary school about creating a volunteer program with seniors. She invited Robert to attend a presentation about the new program. He came, listened, and signed up on the spot. Within 3 weeks, he was volunteering again.

After 6 weeks, Robert told Katrina how happy he was at the school. "I feel good, because I have something to give—I can teach children how to read and write their names!" He has now been working there for many months, and his chattiness has returned. Once again, he is engaged with staff and neighbors at his building. School volunteering lights Robert up, and the staff who knew this worked hard to find the right place for him.

The types of relationships and friendships that are formed with others appear to be linked with gender. As one researcher explained, "Men were likely to meet [friends] at associations and group settings and women through their neighbors."[10] It therefore makes sense that women would be more likely to participate in social activities in their housing communities. This knowledge can help us understand where potential social support may come from.

TRANSGENDER INDIVIDUALS

Gender stereotypes present an even greater challenge for those who identify as transgender. Even within the LGBT community itself, those who are transgender are sometimes ostracized or misunderstood. The uncertainty of where transgender individuals fit into society can lead to confusion and isolation. Thus they may be easy targets of thoughtless jokes or even violence.

For example, some people wrongly believe that a person who is born female and changes genders (a female-to-male, or FTM, transgender man) does so because he wants to "act like a man." There is, however, no single explanation for why some people are transgender. The diversity of transgender expression and experiences argues against any simple or unitary explanation. Many experts believe that biological factors such as genetic influences and prenatal hormone levels, early experiences, and experiences later in adolescence or adulthood may all contribute to the development of transgender identities.[11] People born male and now living as female (male-to-female, or MTF) sometimes have an even harder time presenting their gender as female.[12]

How to Help

1. Help facilitate the formation of a men's peer support group or rap group as well as one for women. When possible, find trained volunteers or leaders to facilitate these groups; such people may have enhanced skills in drawing out participants to feel able to talk freely and nonjudgmentally.

2. Do not assume that when men (or women) say "Everything's fine," that it is actually the case. It may be the case, or they may simply feel the need to remain stoic in front of others. You certainly would never pressure seniors to admit they have needs or issues, but what you can do is respond to their statements in a way that fosters further conversation. Sometimes simply "shooting the breeze" with a resident—talking about the news, their family, or their pets—can be a deeply effective way to build a sense of trust that will likely bring about more frank conversation in the future. When having these "light" conversations, be sure to ask residents their thoughts and opinions whenever it makes sense and be genuinely interested in their responses.

3. It is common for staff to inadvertently set up most site activities as pursuits that traditionally revolve around "women's interests," such as needlework or jewelry making, and many men either are not interested or feel they might be unwelcome in a circle of women. Make sure to identify the interests of male residents by asking them what types of classes or activities they would enjoy or what piques their curiosity. Then provide opportunities for them to act on these interests.

Gender

4. Make sure your site has materials on transgender support groups and other resources, and that such materials are available out in the open. An especially crucial resource to display is the name and address of a trans-friendly clinic or health care practitioner in your area. Contact your local LGBT (lesbian, gay, bisexual, transgender) community center for information about similar services in your area. If you do not have one, contact the national organization SAGE (Services and Action for LGBT Elders; 212-741-2247 or http://www.sageusa.org).

5. On all of your intake forms, be sure to have "transgender" as an option to check in addition to "male" and "female." Some transgender people will not check that box because they identify fully as a man or women, but others may want to check it. Either way, just having it on your forms will show potential transgender residents that they are safe with you and that you are knowledgeable and accepting of the transgender community.

" My cat is the only friend I've had who never gave me bad advice. **"**

—Betty,
Satellite administrator

10

Friendships
and Pets

Our research at Satellite Housing as well as that of others indicates that close relationships with friends can be the most important part of maintaining high levels of contentment and hopefulness. Those who make new friends are healthier and live longer.

As part of its constitution, enacted in 1948, the World Health organization asserted that "Health is a state of complete physical, mental, and social well-being and not merely the absence of disease or infirmity."[1] A 2010 review of 148 studies sought to determine the extent to which social relationships influence risk for mortality, which aspects of social relationships are most highly predictive, and which factors may moderate the risk. Researchers found a 50% increased likelihood of survival for participants with stronger social relationships. This finding remained consistent across age, sex, initial health status, cause of death, and follow-up period.[2]

KEY CONCEPT

As a service provider, you have a strong commitment to the philosophy of individual empowerment—of respecting residents' rights to make their own choices about life, regardless of what others think.

Even with such strong evidence of benefits of social ties, we still see people in our communities who do not have friends and who might even say that they do not want to form close relationships. Despite some residents' reluctance to connect with others, it is important to encourage all residents to try to do so. Now, this is the place where many service providers trip up! As a service provider, you have a strong commitment to the philosophy of individual empowerment—of respecting residents' rights to make their own choices about life, regardless of what others think. That commitment is without a doubt a top priority.

Service providers, however, must discern a delicate line between respecting a person's choice and neglecting to give that person every chance and opportunity possible to develop some type of close connection with another person. Much of the reluctance isolated individuals have toward making new friends comes from past negative experiences. Perhaps they never before experienced a positive or nonmanipulative friendship. Some have had friends pass away and now feel emotionally exhausted at the thought of starting new friendships. So they shy away from what they perceive may be a bad experience.

> "Alzheimer's patients have fewer anxious outbursts if there is an animal in the home."
>
> —Dr. Lynette Hart, Associate Professor, University of California at Davis School of Veterinary Medicine[3]

You can be effective by unobtrusively building trust with these residents. This effort shows the residents that it is possible for them to form a trusting relationship. You can then find out what they are interested in and look for opportunities for socialization that would make sense to each unique person.

Some people might enjoy having a regular visitor to chat with one-on-one. Most communities have organized Friendly Visitor or Senior Companion programs. Some seniors will balk at this type of arrangement because it seems forced to them. For them, instead of "Senior Companion," the visitor can simply be called "a person who plays cards with them twice a month" or "a person who accompanies them around the block every Tuesday." Such an arrangement can be more palatable and still have the same positive social effects. Maybe if they wish, the seniors can teach their companions a few words of another language or help them sharpen their chess skills. *Reciprocity* is very important—even a deal-breaker at times—for some seniors when they agree to connect with a willing visitor.

Other residents might prefer to be in a class or a rap group on a topic that interests them. They might even want to learn improvisation or pick up where they left off in high school and participate in theater performances. Perhaps there is a group of like-minded residents who share the same culture or similar political views who may be interested in meeting regularly as a group. There are as many possibilities as there are people!

Being able to connect with others depends on having the emotional energy and physical ability to visit with one another. As mentioned earlier, poor health and disabilities can contribute to social isolation. These barriers to forming close relationships with others are difficult to overcome, yet they can be lessened by using the telephone or other technology as a means for maintaining and nurturing friendships. For example, the San Francisco Bay Area Senior Center Without Walls is an amazing and wildly successful resource for people who are homebound. It empowers them to reach out and interact while still remaining somewhat anonymous, if they wish, until they are ready to share who they are. People who would ordinarily never reveal their feelings often do so during these telephone rap groups, classes, and celebrations.

PET COMPANIONS AND ANIMAL THERAPY

Pets can bring deep comfort to seniors. In fact, a pet can have the same positive effects as a close friend, including warmth, companionship, and a way for seniors to express their truest feelings to the most objective of listeners.

If a resident does not have the resources or ability to care for a pet, he or she may be interested in helping out with a neighbor's pet or participating in an organized activity such as a pet therapy program. These programs bring pets

Barbara and her pug, Missy, are a delight to spend time with. Missy is about 15 years old and Barbara is 78. As she says, smiling, "I have congestive heart failure, diabetes, and I'm on dialysis three times a week; there's no way I should still be here, but Missy needs me." She talks about how Missy has lost her hearing, moves a little slower than she used to, and how much she loves her. "When I'm feeling bad, she knows it and she comes up to me and looks at me with that sweet little face and I feel better."

Barbara had a second pug named Yoda, who she had adopted 12 years ago after he'd been removed from an abusive home. Yoda died last month and Barbara was incredibly sad and misses him like crazy. To help herself deal with the loss, she created a little corner of the room with his picture, a pillow, and a little clay imprint she designed. Whenever she looks at that, she feels better and knows that Yoda's spirit is still strongly with her and Missy.

Barbara knows Missy is not going to live forever; in fact, she is very realistic about that. But she also knows that when Missy passes, she will still be with her in spirit, just as with Yoda. It is important that Barbara has thought through the loss of her pet; it lays the foundation for coping with the future loss of Missy while still being able to enjoy her in the present every day.

"Pet ownership encourages social interaction with other humans. One study done in a nursing home showed that simply being in the presence of visiting animals appeared to encourage the residents to share personal information about their past and present lives."

—Victoria Aspinall, *The Complete Textbook of Veterinary Nursing*[4]

to the site on a regular basis to give seniors the opportunity to play or cuddle with the animals. Some animal rescue programs offer a variety of opportunities for seniors that are free of charge and that bring animal companionship directly to seniors.

Additionally, some communities have organized "animal socials" during which residents bring their pets for a meet-and-greet with family and friends. As Renae, a service coordinator, explained, "Some of the residents were initially afraid of dogs, but, interestingly, after posing with the animals in photos, they began to develop a liking for them."

When a senior has a deep bond with his or her pet and it dies, the loss can be almost as devastating as the death of a spouse. If this happens, refer to the "How to Help" tips in Section 8 (Intimate Partnerships); many of the tips will be helpful in these situations.

Eddie comes downstairs every day to visit with Cha-Cha, the pet therapy guinea pig that a service coordinator keeps in her office for seniors to cuddle.

How to Help

1. Tap into the local Friendly Visitor or Senior Companion programs in your area. Sometimes it is best to find out what practical needs the seniors may have (such as shopping). Then you can ask the more reluctant residents whether they want someone to help them with their shopping, rather than simply asking whether they want someone to come and talk to them.

2. Seek out extraordinary programs in your area, such as the Senior Center Without Walls, which hosts user-friendly teleconferencing groups for seniors in California (1-877-797-7299; http://www.seniorcenterwithoutwalls.org). Their schedule is packed with everything from depression support groups to New Year's Eve celebrations—all done on the phone together!

3. Establish a buddy system, either with outside volunteers or with residents. Many seniors decide to attend an activity or event because one of their friends is going. This method has proved successful for many seniors. One resident said, "Using a buddy system makes it easier to remember when events are, and it's more fun to go with a friend than by myself."

4. Remind seniors who say they do not want friendships that it is never too late and that friendships can help them stay healthy and experience happiness. Do not force it, but gently, and out of care for each resident, try everything you can to help them form connections with others. Or, when they say they do not want friendships, simply use all the other tools in this list. The word *friendship* never has to come up.

Friendships and Pets

5. Using volunteers, activities coordinators, or adult education teachers, help coordinate various workshops, classes, groups, and committees at your property so that everyone has opportunities to find others with shared interests.

6. Encourage isolated residents who are able to care for a small cat, dog, or guinea pig to acquire such a pet. (But be careful with guinea pigs: They require frequent bedding changes, and some can nip.)

7. Find a local pet visitation program, make it a regular addition to the community's activity calendar, and work with a volunteer to organize your own "pet social." Check out Tony La Russa's Animal Rescue Foundation "People Connect" programs for a great Bay Area example (http://www.tir-arf.org).

8. Get a "house pet" for the community. It can be taken care of by a committee of seniors or by staff. Cats are lower maintenance and should have restrictions on where they wander. You may get one or two people who complain, but most residents will be enthusiastic or neutral. Ensure that their comments are addressed, and absolutely make changes and accommodations if there are any health or safety concerns. Do everything you can to make this happen wherever possible rather than ending a program because of one or two complaints. It is more effective and compassionate to serve the majority.

66 My mechanic told me he couldn't fix my brakes, so he decided to make my horn honk a little louder. **99**

—A joke told to staff by a Satellite resident

11

Transportation

For those lucky enough to have a car, the last thing most of us would want to do is to give up the keys. Our independence would immediately be decreased. Driving is not only a functional, easy way to travel between locations, but also a method to facilitate daily existence and relationships.

Reliable and safe transportation is a vital part of a senior's good life. Without access to a car, older adults need alternative means of transportation to assist in meeting their needs so that they do not begin to isolate themselves. Transportation must not only be reliable and safe, but also easy to use and affordable. Riding a public bus can present a huge obstacle to a senior who might have to stand at a bus stop in all kinds of weather, extract exact change, navigate the steps up, and perhaps deal with a crowded bus while carrying packages. Transportation can become difficult to the point where some seniors end up sacrificing meeting their needs.

66 Reliable transportation for our older adults is vital. If you take away their ability to travel and remain social and active in their community, you take away their freedom and their independence. 99

—Robert K. Pfaff, Executive Director, Akron Metro RTA[1]

The World Health Organization asserts that transportation is a determinant of health because it plays a role in independence and "shapes individuals' access to resources."[2] After they quit driving, many seniors grow significantly less active. Older adults can also feel self-conscious about asking others for rides. About half say that "feelings of dependency" or concerns about "imposing on others" are problems.[4] Seniors want to maintain their independence, and that includes having flexible transportation that suits their needs. Many need help getting in and out of a vehicle or managing walkers or wheelchairs.

Satellite Housing drivers are trained not only to do standard tasks, such as helping to carry grocery bags, but also to actively listen to stories and help riders if they get confused.

And remember, even those seniors who use the bus to tend to basic needs (grocery shopping, medical appointments) might love to occasionally go on a group trip to a flower show or to see the lights around the neighborhood during the holidays. Try to find ways to rent vans or buses to make these socially efflorescent trips happen. The possibility of new friendships being made on these types of trips is high!

SENIORS WHO DO NOT DRIVE HAVE

- 15% fewer trips to the doctor

- 59% fewer shopping trips

- 65% fewer trips for social, family, and religious activities than seniors who drive.[3]

1. Become familiar with your local paratransit, dial-a-ride, or similar program for which residents might be eligible. The application processes can be lengthy, so offer to help residents complete them as they need it.

2. Stay aware of what types of transportation the residents use so that you will know when transitions occur. Residents might lose their licenses due to eyesight problems, or their adult children may have new schedules and be unable to take them shopping anymore. Losing the ability or desire to use various methods of transportation can be a precursor to social isolation.

3. Some cities have organizations that provide volunteers to accompany seniors door-to-door on public transit systems or even to provide volunteer driving.

4. Some areas have "travel training" workshops for seniors to help them navigate their local public transportation systems more easily. This is also something you can ask family members to do for residents.

5. If residents want to go somewhere that has an established community (e.g., to a religious service), help them call the group to see whether anyone lives nearby and can give them a lift.

6. Gather local transit route maps and pamphlets, and distribute them to residents.

Transportation

7. Explore the possibility of starting your own transportation program. The Federal Department of Transportation's web site has periodic requests for proposals, available through your state's 5310 program, to obtain wheelchair-accessible buses. Remember, there are other costs besides the bus itself, including salary, fuel, insurance, registration, and maintenance. (For more details, see http://www.fta.dot.gov/grants/13093_3556.html.)

8. Some senior transportation programs, such as the Independent Transportation Network (ITNAmerica), allow volunteer drivers to bank transportation "credits." The volunteers can then use the credits to pay for their own rides after they stop driving or for rides for a family member. Members also can donate their vehicles and receive credits for future rides. Started in Maine, ITNAmerica now has affiliates in 14 metro areas.

9. Find a nearby assisted-living or continuing care retirement community, most of which have wheelchair-accessible buses, and ask whether they are interested in having some residents ride along. You can discuss how these outings strengthen the community, or invite the administrator to visit your site to get a positive sense of affordable housing.

10. The Beverly Foundation has a wide range of in-depth resources and facts on many aspects of senior transportation, including starting a volunteer driver program (http://www.beverlyfoundation.org/).

"Before I moved in,
I was worried some
people would take
advantage of me
having no relatives.**"**

——Choulas,
Satellite resident

12

New to the Area

Knowing how to get to your usual grocery store is something you probably do not even think about. But remember those times when you had just moved and everything in the neighborhood was a mystery?

Being new to your surroundings, especially if you have mobility issues, can naturally increase the likelihood of social isolation. It can look like an overwhelming, scary world out there when you are not sure how to get from point A to point B. In a survey by Satellite Housing, roughly a fifth of the residents reported being from outside the Bay Area when they arrived at the group's properties. And, of course, all residents are coming to a new home when they first move in.

Staff of residential communities know that those first few days following a move in are a crucial time to connect with new residents. Helping them navigate unfamiliar public transportation systems and giving them tips on where to find the best deal on groceries may seem like small things, but these actions can have a long-lasting impact on how residents feel about their new home and community.

There are many ways you can help residents take those first steps in establishing a social network within their community. Of course, residents have full freedom to decide what, if any, activities they would like to participate in, but service coordinators can encourage this participation through good marketing and personal invitations. By participating in and getting to know their fellow residents during site activities, new residents can begin to feel connected to their new home and neighbors.

One service coordinator created a welcoming committee of current residents to inform new residents of the activities that take place at the building as well as where to go in the neighborhood for various services. This program continues to increase familiarity and allows the new residents to have peers who can help them acclimate to their new environment.

How to Help

1. Keep track of where new residents are coming from. Are they moving from a different city, state, or country? Do they have family or friends nearby?

2. Create a booklet for new residents that lists various grocery stores, restaurants, shopping centers, religious services, and other services nearby. Provide information on how to get to these places. Maps of the area, along with public transportation information, can be critical in connecting seniors to their communities. Providing such information allows residents to feel independent.

3. Establish a welcome committee at your site. They offer a good opportunity for long-term residents to enjoy a more active role in the community. Provide new residents with a contact person they can call on for help in navigating the new environment.

New to the Area

4. Make sure new residents know they are welcome at the coffee hour and other gatherings. It can be intimidating to think about joining a group of people who already know one another well. Be very clear that it is in no way an intrusion by saying, "We love having new faces at the group."

5. If residents are concerned about neighborhood safety, organize a meeting during which they can raise safety concerns and ask questions. Invite the local police or any community policing group to attend. Encourage concerned residents to join a neighborhood watch group.

6. Help residents fill out and send in their updated voter registration forms.

66This is life.
All somebodys
are different.**99**

—Montaha,
Satellite resident

13

Language
and Culture

In focus groups conducted by Satellite Housing, language barriers came up again and again as a challenge that seniors and staff alike experience at their sites. Not knowing how to speak English, however, is not necessarily the crux of the problem. The challenges depend more on the number of other people in a senior's community who speak his or her language and with whom the senior can connect.

KEY CONCEPT

Make no assumptions about how any individual approaches his or her aging and health issues. The key to establishing credibility with residents whose backgrounds differ from yours is to stay receptive and respectfully eager to learn.

A language barrier may also create challenges related to service utilization. It can be daunting to try to make sense of complicated procedures sometimes required to take full advantage of services. Paid interpretation is expensive and, even when it is available, intent often gets "lost in translation." This is one of the toughest obstacles to overcome but, as with many things, a simple increase in staff awareness of the issue can start to counteract potential stumbling blocks.

When we start talking about language, the topics of culture and cultural differences naturally arise as related barriers. Culture can determine how a group thinks about the process of aging or how group members care for their elders. Even the willingness to accept help can differ among groups. For example, in traditional Chinese culture, "individuals—especially women—are not encouraged," according to one researcher, "to disclose their feelings to family members and friends, or to seek professional services when mental problems exist."[1] This is just one of an infinite number of cultural norms one may encounter. Expectations, practices, and behaviors can vary radically.

The following excerpt from a *New York Times* article sums up some of the challenges that arise from language and cultural barriers:

> In California, one in nearly three seniors is now foreign born. Many are aging parents of naturalized American citizens, reuniting with their families. Yet experts say that America's ethnic elderly are among the most isolated people in America. Seventy percent of recent immigrants speak no or little English. Most do not drive. Some studies suggest depression and psychological problems are widespread, the result of language barriers, a lack of social connections, and values that sometimes conflict with the dominant American culture, including those of their assimilated children.[2]

Of course, it is unrealistic to try to learn how aging and illness are approached in all cultures. The important factor, again, is to understand that there often *are* differences. Make no assumptions about how any individual approaches his or her aging and health issues. The key to establishing credibility with residents whose backgrounds differ from yours is to stay receptive and respectfully eager to learn.

The Bay Area city of Fremont has successfully launched the Community Ambassador Program for Seniors (CAPS). The city trains volunteer ambassadors who, as a group, speak twelve languages among them and serve as bridges between the formal network of social services and their respective faith and cultural communities. These ambassadors assist seniors in locating senior services and programs in the city.

Montaha is a quiet, sparkly 71-year-old Persian woman who has been living in Walnut Creek, California, in an independent affordable housing community called Montego Place.

You would never guess it to look at her, but Montaha has lived through some extremely tough times. Married at age 14 to a much older man who, as she says, was usually with his other families, Montaha was left mainly to fend for herself, their six children, and three other children her husband gave to her to raise. All she could do was to focus on her children, caring for them and raising them as best she could. Her struggles developed her ability to survive and are what kept her going.

When Montaha first moved in, she knew no one and few others spoke Farsi, her primary language. But she decided that she would work on her English and introduce herself to other people in the building. Montaha says if someone is rude to her, she has made a conscious decision not to care. And she made friends, lots of them. She helps people with crocheting and also works at the local senior center. The onsite Service Coordinator works closely with Montaha, who loves to translate when she gets the chance as well as help out in other ways. She helped staff plan a multicultural party at the site this year and set up a little table depicting the Iranian New Year along with the traditional foods that are part of the celebration. She taught others how to say words such as *garlic* and *apple* in Farsi, and sang a Persian song for everyone. Montaha was clearly very proud to have been able to share those parts of her life, customs, and ways with her neighbors. And she delighted in learning about her neighbors' traditions as well. She enjoyed learning about Chinese, Russian, and other cultures at the party, saying she felt closer to her neighbors.

Montaha feels people need to make each other happy and help each other. She thrives on helping others. As she herself says, "This is life. All somebodys are different. If someone gets angry or don't understand me, I'm not angry. I get a little sad at first, but then I talk to myself and remember they have problem. I used to have problem; I understand."

DEAF SENIORS

Deaf seniors are at great risk of isolation from support services and social opportunities. The lack of sign language competency in conventional senior housing facilities is a significant barrier to a deaf resident's ability to access services or interact socially. Again, in Fremont, leaders from the deaf community partnered with city officials and Satellite Housing to address this need by creating Fremont Oak Gardens. Built with design elements, amenities, and aging support services for deaf and hard-of-hearing seniors, Fremont Oak

Fremont Oak Gardens, a community designed specifically with deaf seniors in mind.

Gardens is the first and only affordable housing development of its kind in Northern California. Staff includes people from the Deaf Counseling, Advocacy, and Referral Agency (DCARA) who are fluent in sign language. Fremont Oak Gardens has become the unofficial deaf senior center for the Bay Area.

How to Help

1. Recognize the cultural differences in the ways residents handle declining health, and work with them closely to find a system of care that makes sense to them.

2. Offer classes on English as a second language (ESL) through your local adult education programs or from a community or in-house volunteer. These classes can be a fun way to bridge the gap between English and non-English speakers. Language acquisition does not happen overnight, but ESL can provide a sense of community.

3. Learn a few phrases in languages you do not speak, and use them to communicate with residents. It can delight residents if you say "Hello," or "How are you?" and other common phrases in their language. It shows you care enough about the residents to learn more about who they are. Encourage other residents to learn phrases, too.

4. When planning activities and events, especially town hall–type gatherings, try to have a translator so that everyone can participate. Include ASL when necessary. Try using local colleges' work–study programs for a low-cost source of translation.

5. Prepare a binder with picture cards denoting certain common questions and needs. The cards should have words a resident can refer to when making requests. For example, if half the residents speak Mandarin and you only speak English, you might have a card with a picture of a bag of groceries and the words "I need free groceries" written in English and in Chinese. Work with your property manager to develop a similar binder with cards to use for common work orders and other maintenance-related requests.

Language and Culture

6. If you do not speak a resident's language or know American Sign Language (ASL), find organizations and services that target the relevant populations so you can recruit staff that speak or use the unfamiliar language.

7. At least once a year, work with the resident association (if you have one) to organize an intercultural jubilee at your site. Kick off the planning well ahead of time, and suggest that residents bring a dish from their culture to share. Encourage them to don traditional dress, perform a dance or song, and bring mementos, pictures, or culture-specific items they want to share.

8. As you learn of new ways and customs, take pleasure in what you hear. Even if you cannot begin to understand some of them, honor each person's belief and know that it is a piece of the global community of which you are a part. Consider yourself lucky to be allowed glimpses into unfamiliar ways and customs, because it can only broaden your understanding of yourself and, subsequently, your work.

9. Set up an account with a telephone translation service. Although some can be very expensive, a less costly option is CTS Language Link, which provides over-the-phone translation in 150 languages and charges a reasonable per-minute fee (http://www.ctslanguagelink.com).

"We as providers . . .
need to help our
residents by
developing as many
and as varied
opportunities for
civic engagement
as we can.**"**

—Patricia Osage

14

Ideas for
Action

The following pages offer an in-depth look at factors that influence the use of services, as well as some final suggestions for connecting with socially isolated seniors.

CIVIC ENGAGEMENT AND INTERGENERATIONAL PROGRAMS

Many of you who work with seniors have heard the terms *civic engagement* and *intergenerational activity*. They have become buzzwords in the world of aging, and for good reason. But what do they really mean?

Civic engagement is the act of one person helping another person or entity or being involved, on some level, in working for positive change for the community. *Intergenerational activity* involves a person interacting with another person or group of people who belong to a different age group.

These two types of social interaction sound like the basic pieces to everyone's life. For most of us, they are; and for all of us, they should be. More commonly, however, seniors are segregated in the United States through societal norms commonly believed to be helpful and even efficient. The result is that opportunities for intergenerational and civic activities are limited. Society seems to be just waking up to the fact that this approach, while well-meaning, is perhaps not quite as helpful to seniors as originally thought.

People do sometimes have opportunities to help one another and to participate in casual civic engagement, such as checking in on one another, walking a dog when its owner is unable to, or cooking a meal for a neighbor. Informal supports are just as important as anything more organized, and these supports are truly mutually beneficial. We as providers, however, also need to help our residents by developing as many and as varied opportunities for civic engagement as we can. And if these engagements are layered with interactions with people of other ages (babies, kids, teens, young adults), then so much the better.

> "Somehow we have to get older people back close to growing children if we are to restore a sense of community, a knowledge of the past, and a sense of the future."
>
> —Margaret Mead

The societal benefits are significant, including reduced stigma regarding aging, inexpensive help for those in need, healthier seniors, and, therefore, reduced public-dollar expenditures for senior health care. Altruism of all types has been shown to produce positive emotions for the giver. As one researcher asserts, altruism enhances mental and physical health: "Altruism promotes deeper positive social integration, distraction from self-preoccupation, enhanced meaning and purpose, a more active lifestyle, and the presence of positive emotions such as kindness that displace harmful negative emotional states."[1]

The following are examples of some of the many civic-engagement activities seniors can participate in:

- Making quilts for the local children's hospital

- Making needlework projects for a shelter for homeless women and children

- Advocating at the city level for more affordable housing

- Collecting relief funds for a disaster in another country

- Reading in local schools with children identified as at risk

- Teaching other seniors piano, yoga, cooking, or tai chi

- Organizing groups of seniors for regular walks

- Gardening together and hosting potlucks with their harvest
- Playing Nintendo Wii™ video games with kids (often with the kids teaching them how)
- Organizing Halloween parties with a local school
- Participating in rhythm circles for preschoolers
- Helping at the reception desk at their building, at various local senior centers, and at a community center for the deaf
- Helping refurbish computers for public schools through a local technology exchange
- Sorting food at the local food bank
- Volunteering as "senior companions"
- Singing at board and care homes[2]

The Bay Area's StAGEbridge Senior Theater Company is an exemplary organization for both its creative and intergenerational activities (http://www.stagebridge.org). The company uses theater and storytelling to bridge the generation gap by breaking down stereotypes and stimulating more positive attitudes toward aging. StAGEbridge engages in senior theater productions and storytelling in schools, and the company holds acting classes for seniors. Their vision is to nurture cooperation, creativity, and joy among people of all ages and backgrounds.

REMINISCENCE

Research has shown that many people of all ages spend time reminiscing about their past. This activity can serve many helpful purposes, such as working through and resolving

MYTHS AND FACTS ABOUT
INTERGENERATIONAL ACTIVITY:

Myth: You just need to bring young and old people together for
instant intergenerational magic.

Fact: Preparation, planning, and training are necessary for
successful intergenerational programs. Young and old
must be prepared for the experience.

Myth: Older adults are not interested in volunteering with
children and youth.

Fact: Approximately 59% of Americans over age 55 currently
volunteer and say retirement is a time to be active and
involved in the community, to start new activities, and
to set new goals.[3]

Myth: Young people admire people in the media most
(athletes and entertainers).

Fact: When asked to name someone they admire, 18- to-
25-year-olds are twice as likely as older Americans to
name a family member, teacher, or mentor.[4]

past hurts, resentments, or other negative emotions.[5] In particular, reminiscing can help older people prepare for death as they review the whole of their lives and feel satisfaction from their relationships and accomplishments.

Reminiscence, however, can also sometimes lead to focusing too much on the negative aspects of one's past and can thereby result in bitterness, depression, or regret. That is why it is important for those who work with seniors to be aware of people who seem to be "stuck" in negative feelings about their past.

One way to help steer seniors toward an overall positive sense of their lives is to offer an opportunity for them to share those memories—positive and negative—with others who can listen and accept them for who they are and what they have been through in their lifetimes. The reality of human experience is that we all have both positive and negative events in our lives. It is less important what those specific events were and more important that we help people see their lives as an integrated whole—formed of both challenges and triumphs.

This type of sharing can happen in a variety of ways. It can be one-on-one with a senior and a staff person, or it could be through an intergenerational program where younger people meet regularly with seniors to hear their life stories and, perhaps, write it down with or for them, creating a personalized life history book that can be shared with family, if desired. This type of sharing can also occur in a facilitated group setting with structured life review curriculas, which are widely available.

Reminiscence groups can have positive effects not just on individuals but on communities as well, especially in places such as senior housing, where residents are living with people who may seem "different" from one another. In one building, a 10-week reminiscence program brought together a group of residents who, on their own, might not have connected. Over the course of the 10 weeks, members of the group discovered many common histories and interests (e.g., writing, painting, music). The relationships residents developed in the group translated directly into improved interactions among them outside the group. Overall the group interactions enhanced the individual group members' feelings of satisfaction as well as the sense of community in the building. Reminiscence activities have also been used successfully with people in early stages of dementia or Alzheimer's disease.[6]

The following are steps for launching your own reminiscence activity:

- Acquire materials on reminiscence for staff so they can learn some key questions and reflection activities for residents.[7, 8]

- Connect with a local college or high school to find classes where a life-history assignment for students would fit well (English, history, communication studies, psychology). Ask seniors to sign up for a "story partner." Most people love to talk about themselves, and many older people like to "help out" younger people with school assignments.

- Contact a local graduate school in psychology, social work, or counseling to find a facilitator (or someone to co-facilitate with staff) for a life review/reminiscence group on-site. Make sure the students are aware of the warning signs of overnegativity as the group progresses. Proper intervention and support can be provided, if needed.

- Purchase a subscription or two of *Reminisce* magazine for residents to share (http://www.reminisce.com). This magazine can provide a range of entry points for reminiscence, as an individual, as a conversation starter with other seniors, or as a reference point for an invitation to join a reminiscence group.

SPIRITUALITY

Spirituality is the soul—the center—of the human experience. Many seniors embrace some form of it, fine-tuning it within their own belief systems to increasing degrees as they grow older. Spirituality can be a strong coping tool during loss or sickness or when contemplating one's own mortality.

Two aspects of spirituality make it a wonderful tool for preventing isolation. The first is associated solely with one's ideas and credos; spirituality does not necessarily need to be part of a formal religion. It can simply be someone's completely unique take on the meaning of life, the interconnectedness of humankind, or any deeply held belief—whatever anchors that person in such a way that he or she can maintain faith in being alive. This is often the type of thought system that can stave off depression following loss (of others or of abilities) and in turn prompt connection with others.

The other beneficial aspect of spirituality for preventing isolation is faith-based institutions and religious services. For many people these are an important means of sharing mores and identities. They offer a structured place to meet and exchange ideas with people of all ages, and they typically have many opportunities for members to become involved in various committees or projects. If mobility is an issue (and it often is for seniors), work with the seniors to find feasible transportation. Contact the religious institution they wish to visit to see if anyone can give them a lift. Churchgoers will often be glad for the opportunity to help bring someone to a service.

As a side note, but an important one, organized religion often comes with opportunities for touch. Part of the connection we need as human beings is physical contact: to

Senior residents and high school student volunteers play sports on the Nintendo Wii™.

be hugged, to hold hands, to sit cuddled up with someone, to stroke a child's hair or a pet's fur. Too often, however, opportunities for touch disappear for older adults, especially if they have no family. In churches and other spiritual venues, holding hands, placing hands on someone's head, and hugging are commonly part of the ceremony or gatherings that occur after the service.

So do not be afraid to bring up faith, religion, and spirituality to residents and to offer to help with memorial services, meditation groups, or bringing in people from the community who can lead religious studies. Do be careful, of course, not to push any one belief on anyone, and be prepared for those rare individuals who will take offense at the simple mention of a particular religion. Just stay open and assure them that you welcome all walks of spirituality at the community.

TECHNOLOGY

With the decreased ability to rely on public funding for social supports, technologies are increasingly being incorporated into the senior world. For example, Satellite Housing has worked with an agency called WellAWARE to develop a pilot project to install sensory monitoring systems in the homes of some residents. Although this could appear to be the consummate "Big Brother" scenario, it is actually very inobtrusive, has no cameras, and provides information to staff through data interpretation at a central server base. Staff can then talk through anything concerning the resident. They can help residents get in to see their doctor for something that is easily treatable if caught early but potentially dangerous and complicated if left untreated. Some seniors are still wary of this type of system, but many are beginning to understand that it can be invaluable in preventing unnecessary hospitalization.

Some organizations even use cameras in the home, with residents' permission. This remote monitoring provides seniors with a feeling of safety, knowing that whatever happens, someone will know right away. And residents always have the choice to throw a towel over a camera if they want privacy at any given moment.

Video conferencing and video streaming can provide opportunities for all sorts of interactions, including for health purposes, entertainment, or simply shooting the breeze with a friend or grandchild. A staff member or another resident can teach residents how to use the technology, and some of it is free, such as Skype. It may take many lessons, but they can be fun and another way of providing mutually beneficial social interaction.

A terrific government resource is the Eldercare Locator, which offers a publication called "Staying Connected: Technology Options for Older Adults." It is a simple, senior-friendly, six-page guide that explains the basic facts about how to use tools such as Facebook, e-mail, and texting, including privacy and safety information. It also has an introduction to YouTube, Twitter, Skype, instant messaging, and blogging—all tools that seniors can use to stay connected. (Call 1-800-677-1116 for free copies, or get them online at http://www.eldercare.gov.)

Senior Center Without Walls (SCWW) sponsors all sorts of different gatherings and activities for groups of homebound or shy seniors through conference calling on their home phones (see Section 10 for more details). Volunteers go out to seniors' homes and help them get set up for the calls. Lili, 92 years old, participates twice a month in a virtual art group in which folks make art in their homes and talk about their creations with one another. Last year, she was planning to go to her daughter's for Thanksgiving, but her daughter canceled at the last minute. Lili was upset but knew SCWW was hosting a Thanksgiving event, so she joined them. She said they talked about different dishes they had shared with their families over the years, swapped recipes, and told funny stories. Lili had a good time.

It is best when the technological advances are implemented with a strong volunteer program and face-to-face contacts. These programs can put meaning and purpose back into lives, and they will be used more and more with seniors as creative ways to stay connected and safe and to help them live their lives to the fullest.

"If nothing works, do not try to force things, but do still stay in touch with isolated seniors who tell you they do not need anything."

—Patricia Osage

15

Three Final Concepts
to Keep in Mind

There are countless organizations and agencies that provide services for seniors, yet many individuals in need of these services do not use the resources.

One of the basic responsibilities of service staff is to make sure that residents are *aware* of the services. But even when seniors recognize a need for a certain service and know how to apply for it, they still may not use it. Traditions and attitudes toward accepting assistance, services, or programs can vary widely (as addressed in Section 13).

Others may not be willing to accept "charity," or they might think that by doing so they must be incompetent in some way. One researcher explains, "Oftentimes, elderly people do not come forward to demand services because of a sense of stigma as well as a simple lack of know-how necessary for applying for the services."[1] Of course, access is the logistical bridge between seniors and those services. One service coordinator notes that, "Sometimes they don't know the resource exists, and sometimes they know it exists but don't know how to find it. And then other times they know both of those things but need to get there and just can't."

Tips and suggestions on how to help have been provided throughout this book. Here are some final ideas on implementation as well as a summary of the most important things to keep in mind when working with seniors to alleviate isolation. Also included are some troubleshooting tips for when things just do not seem to be moving along. There are no one-size-fits-all solutions. However, a few important themes that come up repeatedly in focus groups are shared here.

❝ One of our residents was very quiet and rarely came to anything, except an occasional bingo game. One day, she happened to come down for bingo and our regular caller wasn't there. This lady says quietly to me, "I used to call bingo for my church; I bet I could call it here." Now our building has a new bingo caller.**❞**

—Troy, an activities coordinator

1. BE PERSISTENT AND DILIGENT.

Instances when profound change is made overnight are rare. Be patient and persistent in a low-key way. Start by simply getting to know the residents in your facility—maybe just a little at first and building relationships over time.

Thinking "There's no rush" would be untrue. Social isolation is an urgent matter. That said, urging yourself to "rush" would not work, either! What does work is to show each individual patience, gentleness, compassion, and genuine interest. Never take a brush-off personally. It is up to the staff member to persevere despite hesitation from the resident.

If nothing works, do not try to force things (that will usually drive someone in the opposite direction), but do still stay in touch with isolated seniors who tell you they do not need anything. Perhaps for several months, you may only be able to get a resident to talk to you about whether the local baseball team won last night or whether he or she thinks it is hot enough out there. Gradually, you will get to know who residents are and begin to understand what might be a good first step for connecting with others—if only by baby steps. If you see such traits as "crankiness" or "extreme shyness" or something else that might be off-putting, remember that the person is a unique human being with a need for connection equal to anyone else's. Over and over, persistence, diligence, and perseverance prove to be the determining factors in whether socially isolated residents get the help they need.

Take a minute and check these things off in your mind if your interaction just does not seem to be going well:

- Is there sincere respect in every word of the interaction?

- Are you laying aside your own agenda for the resident and simply listening to what he or she has to say?

- Would gentle humor break the ice?

- Are you seeing the person as a unique individual rather than as "a client" or "another resident" or "my job"?

- Are you enjoying this very minute—not worried about what will come next or the hundred things you have on your to-do list?[2]

2. GIVE SENIORS EVERY OPPORTUNITY TO GAIN AND EXPAND THEIR SENSES OF PURPOSE AND CONTROL.

"[My service coordinator] never makes phone calls for me or fills out my forms. At first it pissed me off. I figured she was there to work for us, you know? But then she told me she only does that stuff for people who really can't do it because it's good for us to keep our minds sharp."

—A senior resident

People want purpose in, and control of, their own lives. This is true for all age groups. There seems, however, to be a general misconception in the United States that "old people" no longer want or need this control. On the contrary, it is *very* important to allow seniors to make their own decisions and to maintain independence in every possible situation. Service staff are there to provide all of the necessary support, but you have to tread carefully and make sure you are clear about what is truly necessary. It is easy to just "do" for others, but that is usually *not* the most caring approach.

3. GOOD MARKETING AND PARTICIPATORY PLANNING ARE KEY TO SUCCESSFUL WELLNESS PROGRAMS.

The following are some marketing and planning tips to implement in your housing community to engage seniors in events and activities:

- Make flyers with large fonts, high-contrast colors, and with the date, time, and location clearly marked. Have them translated, if possible.

- Do not post flyers too far in advance.

- Personally invite a resident to attend an activity if you think it would help.

- Remind residents of the activity on the day it will happen, and then warmly let them know their presence is welcome.

- Walk residents down from their apartment to the activity the first time or first few times if you think it that might help them attend.

- When setting up presentations, provide snacks, drinks, or something small to take home.

- Ask residents whether they can help the leader of the activity with something concrete associated with the event, such as greeting people, overseeing the sign-in sheet, or setting out the napkins and cups.

- If residents have expressed interest in an activity and you know of a particular resident who might enjoy leading that activity, approach him or her with the possibility.

- Anytime residents express interest in leading a group activity, such as tai chi, painting, language, and so forth, be sure to support them enthusiastically. If they need it, help them find an appropriate venue or assist them with scheduling.

Appendix

QUIZ: KNOWLEDGE OF SOCIAL ISOLATION

1. **What is social isolation?**
   a. Social isolation describes people who live alone.
   b. Social isolation is feeling or being detached from a social network or community.
   c. Social isolation describes people who are limited to the same group of friends.
   d. Social isolation describes people who have fewer than two meaningful relationships.

2. **What factors may put a senior at risk for social isolation?**
   a. Poor health and disabilities
   b. Loss of spouse
   c. Lack of reliable transportation
   d. All of the above

3. **Seniors who are socially isolated are at an increased risk for which of the following?**
   a. Premature death
   b. Depression
   c. Higher stress levels
   d. All of the above

4. **Feeling socially isolated is a normal part of aging.**
   ○ True   ○ False

5. **What would you do to help prevent or alleviate social isolation in a senior?**

Notes

1. INTRODUCTION

1. University of Michigan (2007, October 29). Ten minutes of talking improves memory and test performance. *ScienceDaily*. Available at http://www.sciencedaily.com/releases/2007/10/071029172856.htm.

2. AARP. (2010). Home and community preferences of the 45+ population. Available at http://assets.aarp.org/rgcenter/general/home-community-services-10.pdf.

3. World Health Organization. (2003). The social determinants of health: The solid facts (Second edition). Available at http://www.euro.who.int/__data/assets/pdf_file/0005/98438/e81384.pdf.

3. HEALTH AND DISABILITIES

1. York, E., & Waite, L. J. (2007). Social isolation and health among older adults: Assessing the contributions of objective and subjective isolation. Paper presented at the annual meeting of the American Sociological Association. Available at http://www.allacademic.com/meta/p184840_index.html.

2. Hawkley, L. C., Thisted, R. A., Masi, C. M., and Cacioppo, J. T. (2010). Loneliness predicts increased blood pressure: 5-year cross-lagged analyses in middle-aged and older adults. *Psychology and Aging, 25*(1), 132–141.

3. Shamliyan, T. A., Kane, R. L., Wyman, J., & Wilt, T. J. (2008). Systematic review: Randomized, controlled trials of nonsurgical treatments for urinary incontinence in women. *Annals of Internal Medicine, 148*(6), 459–473.

4. ALZHEIMER'S DISEASE AND COGNITIVE HEALTH

1. Wayne, M. (2009). Signs, symptoms, and stages of Alzheimer's disease. http://www.helpguide.org/elder/alzheimers_disease_symptoms_stages.htm#authors

2. Ramsey, J. (2009). Shy and stressed people more prone to Alzheimer's later in life. *Top News*. Available at http://www.topnews.us/content/22655-shy-and-stressed-people-more-prone-alzheimers-later-life.

3. Doheny, K. (2007). Loneliness may up Alzheimer's risk: Study shows lonely people twice as likely to be diagnosed with the disease. *CBS News.* Available at http://www.cbsnews.come/stories/2007/02/05/health/webmd/main2437045.shtml.

4. *BBC News.* (2009). Staying calm "prevents dementia." Available at http://news.bbc.co.uk/2/hi/7833707.stm.

5. Diamond, M. (1988). Enriching heredity: The impact of the environment on the anatomy of the brain. New York: Free Press.

5. EMOTIONAL HEALTH

1. Author. (2009). Mental Health and the Elderly Position Statement. *American Geriatrics Society.* Available at http://www.americangeriatrics.org/Products/Positionpapers/mentalhl.shtml.

2. Ibid.

3. Browne, J. Positive Aging. (YEAR). Nova Southeastern University. Fischler School of Education and Human Services. Available at http://www.nova.edu/gec/forms/fgcma_positive_aging.pdf.

6. SUBSTANCE USE

1. Chemical dependency and the elderly. Resource Center State of California Alcohol and Drug Programs, Publication No. (ADP) 99-5721. Available at http://www.adp.cahwnet.gov/RC/pdf/5721.pdf

2. Gfroerer, J. C., Penne, M. A., Pemberton, M., & Folsom, R. (2003). Substance abuse treatment need among older adults in 2020: The impact of the baby boom generation. *Drug and Alcohol Dependence, 69*(2), 127–135. Available at http://www.johnstrogerhospital.org/cru/images/education/519cd99e959493c0c6ad6bf40b928794.pdf

3. Han, B., Gfroerer, J. C., Colliver, J. D., & Penne, M. A. (2009). Substance use disorder among older adults in the United States in 2020. Office of Applied Studies, Substance Abuse and Mental Health Services Administration, U.S. Department of Health and Human Services. Addiction, 104(1), 88–96. Available at http://www.doctordeluca.com/Library/AbstinenceHR/SubstanceUseDisordersIn2020-09.pdf

7. HOARDING

1. Jacobson, S. (2008, September). Hoarding: When Stuff Takes Over a Life. Presentation at the National Service Coordinators Conference.

2. eSMMART. (2008). Hoarding 101: Behind Closed Doors: Getting a Handle on Hoarding. Available at http://www.caring.com/static/hoarding_101.pdf.

3. Steketee, G., & Frost, R. O. (2007). *Compulsive Hoarding and Acquiring.* New York: Oxford Press.

8. INTIMATE PARTNERSHIPS

1. Social isolation: Strategies for connecting and engaging older people. Cornell Institute for Translational Research on Aging (CITRA). Available at http://www.citra.org/Assets/documents/Social%20Isolation.pdf.

2. Integrating lesbian, gay, bisexual, and transgender older adults into aging policy and practice. Public Policy Report by National Academy on an Aging Society, Volume 21, No. 3 (Summer 2011). Available at http://www.sageusa.org/uploads/PPAR%20Summer20111.pdf.

3. HUD proposes new rule to ensure equal access to housing regardless of sexual orientation or gender identity. Press release from the Department of Housing and Urban Development (January 20, 2011). http://portal.hud.gov/hudportal/HUD?src=/press/press_releases_media_advisories/2011/HUDNo.11-006

9. GENDER

1. Aday, R. H., Kehoe, G. C., & Farney, L. A. (2006). Impact of senior center friendships on aging women who live alone. *Journal of Women & Aging, 18*(1), 57–73.

2. Kochanek, K. D., Xu, J., Murphy, S. L., Miniño, A. M., & Kung, H.-C. (2011). Deaths: Preliminary data for 2009. *National Vital Statistics Reports, 59*(4). National Center for Health Statistics. Available at www.cdc.gov/nchs/data/nvsr/nvsr59/nvsr59_04.pdf.

3. Cohn, D., Passel, J., Wang, W., & Livington, G. (2011). Barely half of U.S. adults are married: A record low new marriages down 5% from 2009 to 2010. Available at http://www.pewsocialtrends.org/2011/12/14/barely-half-of-u-s-adults-are-married-a-record-low/

4. Johnson, C. L., & Barer, B. M. (1996). *Life beyond 85 years: The Aura of Survivorship*. New York: Springer.

5. Social isolation in seniors: An emerging issue. An investigation by the Children's, Women's and Seniors Health Branch, British Columbia Ministry of Health. March 2004. Available at http://www.health.gov.bc.ca/library/publications/year/2004/Social_Isolation_Among_Seniors.pdf.

6. Male stoicism: Bad for the health. Johns Hopkins Medicine Healthy Living alert, posted November 23, 2011. Available at http://www.johnshopkinshealthalerts.com/alerts/healthy_living/male-stoicism_5908-1.html.

7. National Institute of Mental Health. (2009). Suicide in the U.S.: Statistics and prevention. Available at http://www.nimh.nih.gov/health/publications/suicide-in-the-us-statistics-and-prevention/index.shtml.

8. Centers for Disease Control and Prevention, National Center for Injury Prevention and Control. Web-based Injury Statistics Query and Reporting System (WISQARS). Available at http://www.cdc.gov/ncipc/wisqars.

9. Oquendo, M. A., Ellis, S. P., Greenwald, S., Malone, K. M., Weissman, M. M., & Mann, J. J. (2001). Ethnic and sex differences in suicide rates relative to depression in the United States. *American Journal of Psychiatry, 158*(10), 1652–1658.

10. Johnson C. L., & Barer, B. M. (1996). Life beyond 85 Years: The Aura of Survivorship. New York: Springer.

11. American Psychological Association. Answers to your questions about transgender people, gender identity, and gender expression. Available at http://www.apa.org/topics/sexuality/transgender.aspx#.

12. Kruijver Frank, P. M., Zhou, J. N., Pool, C. W., Hofman, M. A., Gooren, L. J., & Swaab, D. F. (2000). Male-to-female transsexuals have female neuron numbers in limbic nucleus. *Journal of Endocrinology & Metabolism, 85*(5), 2034–2041.

10. FRIENDSHIPS AND PETS

1. World Health Organization (WHO). (1948). WHO's constitution was adopted by the International Health Conference held in New York from June 19 to July 22, 1946, signed on July 22, 1946, by the representatives of 61 states, and entered into force on April 7, 1948.

2. Holt-Lunstad, J., Smith, T. B., Layton, J. B. (2010). Social relationships and mortality Risk: A meta-analytic review. *PLoS Medicine* 7(7). Available at e1000316. doi:10.1371/journal.pmed.1000316.

3. Davis, J. L. (2009). 5 ways pets can improve your health. Available at http://www.webmd.com/hypertension-high-blood-pressure/guide/5-ways-pets-improve-your-health.

4. Aspinall, V. (2006). *The Complete Textbook of Veterinary Nursing.* Oxford: Butterworth-Heinemann.

11. TRANSPORTATION

1. Bailey, L. (2004). Aging Americans: Stranded without options. Surface Transportation Policy Project. http://www.transact.org/report.asp?id=232.

2. British Columbia Ministry of Health. (2006). Social isolation among seniors: An emerging issue. http://health.gov.bc.ca/library/publications/year/2004/Social_Isolation_Among_Seniors.pdf.

3. Bailey, L. (2004). Aging Americans: Stranded without options. Surface Transportation Policy Project. http://www.transact.org/report.asp?id=232.

4. Ritter, A., Straight, A., & Evans, E. (2002). Understanding senior transportation: A report and analysis of a survey of consumers age 50+. AARP Public Policy Institute report #2002-04. http://assets.aarp.org/rgcenter/il/inb50_transport.pdf.

13. LANGUAGE AND CULTURE

1. Smith, A. L. (2006). Thriving not surviving: Meeting the needs of seniors in poverty: Service utilization and quality of life in three types of senior housing. Saint Mary's College of California: 8.

2. Brown, P. L. (2009). Invisible immigrants, Old and left with "no one to talk to." *New York Times*. August 31. Available at http://www.nytimes.com/2009/08/31/us/31elder.html.

14. IDEAS FOR ACTION

1. Pang, S. (2009). Is altruism good for the altruistic giver? *The Dartmouth Undergraduate Journal of Science*. Available at http://dujs.dartmouth.edu/spring-2009/is-altruism-good-for-the-altruistic-giver.

2. Generations United. (2007). The benefits of intergenerational programs: Fact sheet. Available at http://www.gu.org/RESOURCES/Publications.aspx.

3. Glass, T. A., Freedman, M., Carlson, M., et al., (2004). Experience corps: Design of an intergenerational program to boost social capital and promote health. *Journal of Urban Health 81*(1), pp. 94–105.

4. The Pew Research Center for the People and the Press. (2007). A portrait of "Generation Next": How young people view their lives, futures and politics. Available at http://www.people-press.org/2007/01/09/a-portrait-of-generation-next/.

5. McKee, K., Bolton, G., Chung, M. C., Goudie, F., Wilson, F., & Elford, H. (2003). Evaluating the impact of reminiscence on the quality of life of older people. Available at http://www.growingolder.group.shef.ac.uk/KevinMcKee.htm.

6. Kennard, C. (2006). Reminiscence therapy and activities for people with dementia. Available at http://alzheimers.about.com/cs/treatmentoptions/a/reminiscence.htm.

7. The Benevolent Society. (2006). Reminiscing handbook. Available at http://www.bensoc.org.au/director/resources.cfm?action=search&keyword=reminiscing+&resourcetype=&resourcesubject=&submit.x=0&submit.y=0.

8. McLean, V. (2003). Time to remember: Introducing reminiscence into elderly care. Ledbury, United Kingdom: Elderly Care Books. Available at http://elderlycarebooks.co.uk/index.html.

15. THREE FINAL CONCEPTS TO KEEP IN MIND

1. Choi, N. G. (1994). Patterns and determinants of social service utilization: Comparison of the childless elderly and elderly parents living with or apart from their children. *The Gerontologist, 34*(3): 353–362.

2. Thanks to Josiah Polhemus of StAGEbridge for inspiring this list with his "Reach" method. http://stagebridge.org/.